ADVANCE PRAISE

"*I wish I could have read this book before I became the head of Global eBusiness at P&G! The 6 P's of implementing a digital analytics transformation is an extremely comprehensive and valuable framework. No matter where you are in your journey—crawl, walk, or run—the key is to get your learning flywheel spinning to create a continuous and cumulative advantage over time.*"

—FD WILDER, SENIOR ADVISOR AT MCKINSEY
& COMPANY AND FORMER P&G SVP

"*While nearly all large companies have an enterprise-level analytics platform, only the best understand how to get value out of it. Crawl, Walk, Run will help you reach that critical stage.*"

—VERNE HARNISH, AUTHOR OF *SCALING UP* AND
MASTERING THE ROCKEFELLER HABITS

"*Michael and Alex have been on the cutting edge of marketing analytics for over a decade. This book is a must-read for marketing and analytics professionals at all levels. Real, usable insights.*"

—CAMERON HEROLD, AUTHOR OF *VIVID
VISION* AND *MEETINGS SUCK*

CRAWL, WALK, RUN

CRAWL
WALK
RUN

EDITION II

Advancing Analytics Maturity
with Google Marketing Platform

MICHAEL LOBAN
ALEX YASTREBENETSKY
OF INFOTRUST

LIONCREST
PUBLISHING

CRAWL, WALK, RUN
Advancing Analytics Maturity with Google Marketing Platform

SECOND EDITION

ISBN   978-1-5445-2019-3 *Hardcover*
        978-1-5445-2018-6 *Paperback*
        978-1-5445-2020-9 *Ebook*

To my wife, Karina, and my children, Ilya, Maria, and Anna, who put up with my ten years of learning that went into writing this book.

To my parents, Mikhail and Lidiya, who gifted me with an insatiable hunger for education, a high work ethic, and a passion for sharing what I've learned with others.

To Michael, who is so much more for me than just my coauthor.

To the entire InfoTrust team and our amazing partners, who have provided me with an incredible experience that I am excited to share in this book.

To the many more miracles we will get to create by donating 100 percent of the sales of this book to the InfoTrust Foundation.

Grateful,
Alex

For my family and the InfoTrust team, who helped make this possible.

Michael

CONTENTS

DISCLAIMER

The information covered in this book is not intended to be legal advice or counsel. You should not act or refrain from acting on the basis of any content included in this book regarding legal compliance without first seeking legal advice. The contents of this book contain general information related to applicable laws but may not reflect your current situation. We disclaim all liability for actions you take or fail to take based on any content in this book. Any action you perform as a result of the information provided in this book is at your own discretion.

VISIT THE BOOK COMPANION WEBSITE NOW

To get the most out of *Crawl, Walk, Run: Advancing Analytics Maturity with Google Marketing Platform*, we encourage you to visit infotrust.com/crawl-walk-run/ as you read. This companion site has complementary and exclusive resources that will enrich your reading experience. Many of these resources can also be shared with your colleagues.

In this book, you won't find the names of any of our forty-plus Fortune 500 partners or our major publishing and retail clients. We have too much respect for our clients to violate their trust and publicly share their names. However, our companion site contains links to many of our branded and anonymous case studies.

The InfoTrust team will continue to update the infotrust.com/ crawl-walk-run website with additional resources, articles, and case studies.

FOREWORD

BY SEAN DOWNEY, VP, MEDIA PLATFORMS, GOOGLE

The past year has increased the need for businesses to embrace digital transformation so they can be better prepared for whatever the future brings. The COVID-19 pandemic impacted businesses everywhere, with some verticals, like travel, hit harder than others. Every marketer faced the challenge of understanding and responding to rapidly-changing customer demand. Existing digital trends also accelerated. For example, the growth of online ordering with store pickup and the shift to connected TV happened even faster than anticipated. Taken together, this all means that there are significant, lasting changes in customer behavior that your business will need to address.

Of course, there are other industry changes—driven by rising consumer expectations for privacy—that can pose challenges for marketers and require new ways of approaching digital marketing. New regulations have set higher standards for user privacy and data protection. Browsers and mobile operating systems have announced, or implemented, new policies that limit many of the techniques used in digital marketing today. At Google, we believe we can improve the user experience across the internet, *and* have users feel confident their privacy is protected, while still preserving advertiser performance. For our industry, it's an opportunity to reinvent digital marketing and measurement while putting users first.

Even with all these changes, I'm seeing marketers rise to these challenges by investing in digital transformation and embracing new technology and data strategies. My team at Google has been pleasantly surprised by how leaned-in our customers have been in using this moment to further transform and innovate their businesses.

A custom printing company found that their small business customers needed less of their traditionally popular items, like swag for trade shows. They responded by increasing marketing for rising categories, like in-store signage, and by launching new business lines, like custom masks. Investing in digital analytics helped them understand these customer behavior changes quickly and enabled them to monitor and optimize their new marketing campaigns.

A global cosmetics brand used insights from digital analytics combined with cloud-based machine learning to predict which customers would be most likely to purchase. They then used these predictive audiences to reach those customers with advertising campaigns. As a result, they saw a growth in sales and improved return on ad spend.

Now's the time to build the digital foundation your business needs to succeed. Your analytics strategy is key to this success. With more commerce moving online and businesses under increased pressure to make every marketing dollar count, insights from digital analytics tools are critical. Analytics insights help you understand customer preferences and create better experiences for them. And you get a more complete picture of the many, rapidly changing ways customers interact with your business, whether it's on the web or an app, so you can respond effectively.

We recently introduced the new Google Analytics to give your business the essential insights you need to be ready for what's next. It has machine learning at its core to automatically surface helpful insights and gives you a complete understanding of your customers across devices and platforms. And it's privacy-centric by design, so you can rely on Analytics even as industry changes, like restrictions on cookies and identifiers, create gaps in your data.

This book will serve as a great guide for you and your business as you evaluate your analytics strategy. There are valuable things you can learn whether you're new to Google Analytics or looking for help with advanced use cases.

From my experience, there are a few things to consider as you begin this journey.

First, **keep your focus on your customer.** As you invest in new areas, like better collecting and using first-party data, make the customer experience central to your strategy. It's especially important to keep privacy top of mind and give your customers choice and control over the data they choose to share.

Think long-term. While every business is facing urgent needs, resist the urge to switch to short-term goals and metrics. Use this time to invest in the future. For example, put in place structural upgrades to your analytical capabilities and train your people on new analytical skills.

Finally, remember that **failing is okay.** Embrace an explorer mindset and seek new ways of doing things. Cultivate a culture that believes in progress, not perfection. Tolerating failures and appreciating the lessons learned from experiments that didn't work makes you wiser and better prepared for the future.

Looking forward to a transformational year ahead.

—SEAN DOWNEY

INTRODUCTION TO THE SECOND EDITION

A couple of years ago, I (Alex) attended the Google Partners summit alongside a number of our clients and advertisers. Google had just announced Universal Analytics, which represented a major shift for Google Analytics. There was a lot of excitement in the crowd about what the new platform had to offer, but also a fair amount of trepidation about the change.

After the main session, we participated in breakout sessions to learn more about the specific features and functionality of Universal Analytics. At one of those sessions, I began chatting with the director of analytics for a major client company about the process of migrating to Google's new solution. She seemed concerned about what it was going to take to migrate.

"Since custom variables are going away," she said, "and Google is replacing them with custom dimensions, which work very differently, does that mean we'll have to redo our architecture?"

"I'm afraid so," I replied. "This is what we will need to do to properly migrate to Universal Analytics."

At that time, I heard many questions like these from concerned business leaders. Universal Analytics offered a lot of new possibilities for advanced analytics, but the process of migration seemed daunting.

With Google's release of Google Analytics 4 (GA4), I am feeling a sense of déjà vu, as I receive multiple calls each week from leaders of major businesses, including some Fortune 500 companies, asking me about deploying GA4. They want to know how it's going to impact tracking, billing, and so much more. You may be wondering the same thing.

THE GROWING PAINS OF INNOVATION

In this second edition of *Crawl, Walk, Run*, we've included a lot of new content on Google Analytics 4, so we can share with you what the new platform has to offer, as well as what the transition is going to entail. GA4 is a prime example of how Google is at the forefront of analytics innovation, inspiring organizations to think in new ways. They're not afraid to disrupt the industry because they know that this monumental leap in analytics will make things better for everyone.

Incremental improvements alone aren't enough. While Google has excelled at incremental innovation over the years, they also realize that sometimes, you have to take a leap toward disruptive change, even if that means companies are going to experience some "growing pains." Even with the challenges brought about by the changes in GA4, migration is still the right thing to do because of what it's going to mean for the future of analytics.

There are essentially three kinds of innovation that companies can pursue. First, there is *core innovation*, which means investing in the things the company is already doing well. This might include scaling processes that are already effective in order to provide a greater return. The second is *emerging innovation*, which means investing in things that have shown some promise for the organization. Typically, these things will need a significant amount of time and resources in order to be fully realized in the company. The final type is called *new innovation*, which means investing in the wild and crazy ideas that smart people in the organization are experimenting with.

Eric Schmidt, CEO of Google from 2001 to 2011, famously said that Google followed a 70, 20, 10 allocation model: 70 percent of their resources go toward core innovation, 20 percent toward emerging innovation, and 10 percent toward the new stuff. Google Analytics 4, in a sense, represents all three kinds of innovation in one incredible new platform. Yes, there are going to be challenges when migrating to GA4, but any company that wants to stay ahead of the curve—not just crawling, but running toward greater success with their digital marketing—must be willing to do some things that might be uncomfortable.

The question you need to ask yourself is this: "What changes do we need to put in place *now* in order to get where we want to go with digital analytics in three or four years?" Indeed, this is a question we often confront clients with when we meet with them because if you know where you want to go, then you'll be more willing to endure some discomfort to get there.

Consider how a little discomfort now might impact your position on the road to success in the months and years to come. The good news is that adoption of GA4 won't hurt your current analytics. That's because it can be deployed on a website without sacrificing your current tracking. So, you have one less reason to wait! Indeed, if you wait too long to make the change, you might find yourself falling behind.

In fact, one of the reasons why we decided to write a second edition of this book so quickly is to get ahead of the curve and share answers to the questions that we are anticipating. Our answer to your unspoken question is clear. Yes, migrating to Google Analytics 4 is the right thing to do, no matter how challenging it might seem.

This next iteration of Google Analytics is coming, possibly sooner than you realize, so we've included updated information, along with an entirely new chapter, so this book can serve as an up-to-the-minute guide for your company in moving toward digital analytics maturity. Indeed, when it came to publishing this second edition, we took our own advice: make the change sooner rather than later, even if it's challenging.

Additional information about migrating to Google Analytics 4 can be found on our website at https://infotrust.com/crawl-walk-run/, where we've put together webinars, videos, and deep dives on a range of relevant topics. This is a *big* change, and we know that in a large organization, major changes take time. Hopefully, we've gotten this information into your hands soon enough that you can begin preparing now for what Google R&D has planned in the coming months.

EMBRACE THE FUTURE RIGHT NOW

Soon, you will have access to amazing capabilities. We want you to start exploring the possibilities now, getting your hands dirty so when GA4 launches, you're already beyond the "crawl" phase of its adoption, ready to take these new capabilities and run with them.

There are some things coming that we can't even share publicly, but take our word for it—it's going to be amazing. Don't wait to see how things play out with GA4. Start piloting this new technology as soon as possible. Get comfortable with what's coming, so you can make the most of it when it arrives. We strongly encourage you to embrace the future right now because Google Analytics 4 *is* the future, and the future for digital analytics looks amazing.

INTRODUCTION TO THE FIRST EDITION

It was July 2012, and Alex and I had scheduled an interview with Google to become a certified partner. We had already gone through a complex process, submitted paperwork and case studies, and the phone call was the last step. The morning of the interview, Alex and his wife had a doctor's appointment. She was pregnant and one day past her due date. During the appointment, the doctor decided to conduct an ultrasound, and based on the results of the ultrasound, he would determine whether or not to induce labor.

After the ultrasound, she said, "You're not going home. This baby will be delivered today." As Alex's wife was checked into the hospital, Alex made a few calls to let friends and family know. When he called me, I gently reminded him, "You know our Google certification interview is today, right?"

We were so anxious about getting this certification that I decided to come to the hospital. Doing a conference call did not even occur to us; we figured we could conduct the interview by phone in the waiting room. Consequently, I drove straight to the hospital to meet Alex on the OB floor. As the time for our interview drew near, Alex kept going back and forth between the delivery room and waiting room.

Finally, the Google Partner Manager called, and the interview began. First, he asked a series of business and marketing questions, which I handled with no problem. Then he began asking technical questions. This is more of Alex's area of expertise, but as he attempted to answer them, he found himself stumbling over his words. The longer it took, the more anxious he got. With the impending birth of his child, he just couldn't think about analytics.

The clock was ticking. The baby was due to be born within the next hour or two. It was too much, and Alex realized the time had come to share what was happening.

"Look, I'm sorry," he said, "but we're currently sitting outside of the delivery room where my wife is being induced. My first child will be born any minute now, but we're so committed to becoming a Google partner that we just didn't want to reschedule the interview. It's too important to us. However, I'm having trouble formulating my answers, so if you want to email me some questions, I promise the guys will get back to you while I am here."

It was a risky move, but the Google Partnership Manager said, "I appreciate your dedication. I'll get back to you in a few days." And that was the end of the call. We had no idea what was going to happen next. Fingers crossed, Alex headed back into the delivery room to be with his wife. His son was born a couple of hours later.

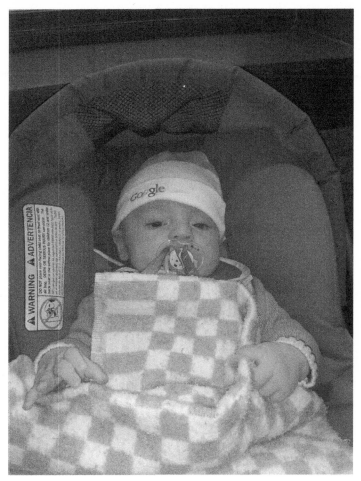

A picture of Alex's son, Ilya.

A few days later, we received the news: our company had been approved. The foundation was laid for InfoTrust to become one of the largest privately owned Google partners in the country. Six months later, we became one of the first resellers of what was then called Google Analytics Premium.

Since then, our organization has been fortunate to work with over forty Fortune 500 companies and some of the largest retailers in the world, helping them implement analytics worldwide across thousands of websites. In doing so, we have seen the struggles leaders have in navigating the marketing technology landscape, a struggle that is exacerbated by a singular problem: there are far too many choices!

Every year, the MarTech Conference releases an updated infographic showing the entire marketing technology landscape. As of 2019, the infographic includes over 7,000 different products. It's such a complex and convoluted list, it is eye-straining to take it all in.[1]

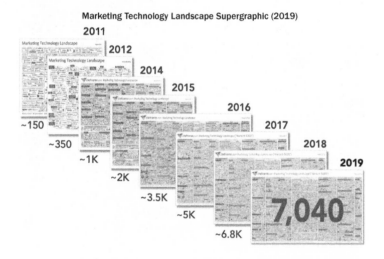

Marketing Technology Landscape Supergraphic (2019)

How in the world can a new leader in a digital marketing organization begin to decipher which tech products are best going to meet their needs? Even with the right products, aligning people, processes, and platforms to achieve digital analytics maturity can seem like a daunting prospect.

1   Scott Brinker, "Marketing Technology Landscape Supergraphic (2019): Martech 5000 (actually 7,040),"
      April 4, 2019, https://chiefmartec.com/2019/04/marketing-technology-landscape-supergraphic-2019/.

WHY "CRAWL, WALK, RUN?"

Change is inevitable, but progress is optional. When it comes to digital analytics, as in all things in life, problems are going to arise. Even now, as of the writing of this book, we see many organizations filing for bankruptcy as a result of the unforeseen economic fallout from quarantines and social distancing: J. Crew, 24 Hour Fitness, and many others are going out of business. Change happens whether we want it or not, but progress is the result of intentional decisions made within an organization.

However, progress doesn't happen overnight. It's a process that occurs gradually, one smart decision at a time. We have called this book *Crawl, Walk, Run* to emphasize this point. When it comes to digital transformation in your organization, it's going to take time and effort.

Of course, every organization wants their analytics to suddenly be complete and thorough, optimizing customer data with scientific precision, but you have to learn to crawl before you can learn to walk, and you have to learn to walk before you can learn to run. In other words, you have to start making consistent, incremental progress before you can become fully proficient at digital analytics. We will introduce you to a couple of models that will help your organization plan and achieve that progress.

The world of analytics is far too complex, and without a practical guide, it can be nearly impossible to figure out how to get where you need to go. In this book, we want to provide that practical guide, using a foundational platform that you probably already have: Google Marketing Platform. After all, Google Analytics is the most popular analytics service in the world, comprising 85.3 percent of the market.[2]

In the following chapters, we will show you how to create a beautiful analytics setup that will clarify the road ahead, and we'll look at the different stages of analytics maturity so you can clearly outline what your organization needs to do for some quick wins at each stage. You'll know how to avoid overpriced analytics projects that consume too many years and too much money. Instead, you'll be able to transform your organization in stages with greater efficiency, making the company more profitable through the use of analytics at every stage of maturity.

We will show you how to get the most out of the Google Marketing Platform, maximizing the value for your teams and your organization as a whole. Through our experience with companies around the world, we have developed a few key frameworks that will help you quickly and easily figure out where you are and where you need to go, enabling you to map out the transformation of your organization.

The processes we take you through have worked extremely well for our clients, and while we won't share any confidential client information, we do intend to share as much as we can to make your life as a digital executive easier.

But before we work on where we need to go, we need to know where we are now. To do that, we need to know the current lay of the land, which we'll explore in the next chapter.

As we get started, now is a great time to visit infotrust.com/

---

2   "Usage Statistics and Market Share of Google Analytics for Websites," *W3 Techs*, https://w3techs.com/technologies/details/ta-googleanalytics/all/all (accessed January 5, 2020).

crawl-walk-run, the companion site for this book. There you will find complementary and exclusive resources that will help you get even more value out of this book.

PART ONE

• • • •

WHERE ARE YOU NOW?

CHAPTER ONE

THE LAY OF
THE LAND

December is typically a quiet month for us. Most companies have already allocated their budgets for the year and spent what they intended to spend on digital marketing analytics. Furthermore, the last two weeks of the month tend to be when people take time off for holidays and visiting family, so we generally don't have meetings scheduled.

But one year, things were different. A new director of marketing at a retail brand in Ohio contacted us through a mutual business acquaintance and invited us to her office. Though it was the middle of December, she wanted to make early progress in her new position.

As we walked into the office space, we were surprised at how open and empty it seemed. Everything looked clean and bright with a beautiful view overlooking the city, but there were hardly any employees. When we met with the client, we asked, "Is everyone on location somewhere?"

"No," she replied. "This is a new floor for our company. Our goal is to eventually fill this space. We want to hire data analysts and data scientists, and we want to fully build out all of our analytical capabilities in-house. That's why I invited you here today. Maybe this is a good opportunity for our companies to work together."

It sounded great, but during the meeting, we started to hear her ideas for her organization. She wanted better measurements, more personalization; she was interested in cloud storage—all fairly standard things that organizations think about when planning their digital transformation. As she wrote all of the things she wanted on a whiteboard, it began to look like a kid's Christmas wish list—timely, considering it was December—but one key thing was missing from the list: *why*.

Why did they want these things? Why did they believe these things would improve their customer experience?

When organizations think about digital transformation, they tend to think: "We need to collect more. We need to analyze data better. We need to personalize information better. Then we can figure out what we need to do as an organization." In other words, they believe analytics and better data will clarify their purpose. We believe that's the wrong place to start.

Instead of creating a wish list of what your organization wants, start with the customer experience. What does the *customer* want? What are they missing that would dramatically improve their lives, and how can you create it for them? Once you understand the customer experience you are trying to create, you can craft a road map that will help you construct and implement it. Rather than simply piling up massive amounts of analytics data, you will be able to prioritize your analytics initiatives and leverage data through the lens of *purpose*, focusing your analytics efforts in a pointed way that will get you where you need to be *for the customer's sake.*

Of course, doing things for the customer's sake often requires us to disrupt ourselves. John Chambers, former CEO of Cisco, under whose leadership the company grew exponentially, says that if disruption isn't at the core of your strategy, you have a problem. When you compete against other companies, you're looking backward. However, when you compete against the market transition, you learn to see around corners.

Ironically, when the retail brand we mentioned at the beginning of the chapter became our client, we managed to accomplish every single thing that was on their wish list, but we did it all through the lens of how it would improve the day-to-day experience of their clients.

WHY DIGITAL TRANSFORMATIONS FAIL

We've seen far too many digital transformations fail. Executives have unrealistic expectations about what digital transformation and analytics can accomplish for them. They aren't a cure-all, but leaders are convinced that if they get better data, it will make a drastic improvement within their organization. It doesn't always work out that way. On the contrary, we've seen companies chase analytics right into bankruptcy.

There are a few key reasons why digital transformations sometimes fail.

First, leaders lack clarity about *what they are trying to accomplish* with the data. Increasing the conversion rate on your website is not enough reason to commit to a digital transformation. If you're not doing it specifically to serve your customers better, then it's probably not going to be very fruitful. For that reason, you need clear, measurable objectives and KPIs. Otherwise, how will you know when you've successfully transformed?

Second, companies often start collecting data, but individual teams within the organization each use their own reports and data points. It's not enough to have access to analytics data. Everyone needs to be on the same page, using the same key data points to ensure that all teams are unified and working with a shared vision.

For example, Dominos, the popular pizza chain, has said that their number one goal is to create the best online ordering experience in the industry. Since so many customers order online, they want the process to be fast, easy, and pleasant. They have been able to use analytics data to help them achieve this singular, unified goal. Using the full power of data, they've delivered on their ideal experience and greatly increased their market cap.[3]

Third, there is often a lack of follow-through from executives. The CEO or executive team might think analytics initiatives are important now, but will transformation still be a priority in twenty-four months? If digital transformation doesn't become part of your organization's DNA, if it doesn't change the way your people operate on a daily basis, they will fall back to their past behavior.

---

3   Suman Bhattacharyya, "Domino's In-House Technology Push Has Helped Increase Online Orders," *Digiday*, October 17, 2018, https://digiday.com/retail/dominos-house-technology-push-helped-increase-online-orders/.

The nature of technology today has made it easier than ever for small startups to come in and disrupt your space because the barrier to entry is lower. To compete, you have to implement new processes that allow for continuous organizational transformation. Otherwise, you will be eaten alive. In that sense, digital analytics is a necessary piece of an overall strategy for staying relevant in the face of industry disruption.

The entire world is trying to understand what the new norm for eRetail is going to be. There is no dataset that can predict the certainty or success of digital transformation initiatives, but we believe that continuous innovation is going to become the new norm. Leaders will have to dust off their copies of *Lean Startup* and, especially, *The Startup Way* (both by Eric Ries) and learn how to establish a hypothesis, figure out what data they need to test and validate, or fail fast.

IT'S TIME TO FOCUS

Let's suppose you're the new director of marketing, and you've been brought on board to implement digital transformation within an organization. Or perhaps you've been tasked with deploying and ensuring the adoption of Google Marketing Platform across your organization. There are so many different analytics topics to think about and so many different data points to be mindful of; how can you focus and start making progress?

As we speak at conferences and meet with business leaders, we've encountered hundreds of organizations that are in this situation. To start making progress, we believe there are a few key analytics topics that you should focus on. We'll look at them briefly now and then dive deeper later.

Specifically, we recommend focusing on customer data governance, building in-house digital capabilities, attribution/media mix modeling, and leveraging data at scale with Cloud for Marketing. While we are primarily discussing how to achieve marketing maturity with Google Marketing Platform, the concepts explained in the following sections can be applied to any digital analytics transformation.

CUSTOMER DATA GOVERNANCE

For years, a kind of abuse has been rampant in almost every industry in regard to customer data. Companies have collected data from their customers without informing them about: 1) what data was being collected, and 2) what was being done with that data.

A couple of years ago, I was in Dubai to speak on a panel about analytics as a competitive advantage. One of the attendees raised her hand and asked, "What should we do about collecting customer information that we don't need right now?"

A panelist sitting next to me replied, "Collect as much data as you can, regardless of what you do with it. Putting data in the cloud is cheap. You can figure out what to do with it later."

Can you imagine if you went into a store and just bought a bunch of random stuff you didn't need, brought it all home, and dumped it in an empty room? "I'll just buy as many things as I can, whether I need them or not, because they're cheap, and I have plenty of space." That's how companies have treated customer data. They don't even know what to make of most of the information, but they collect it because they can. Furthermore, they use it however they want, if they use it at all.

Governments have begun putting a stop to this practice by introducing increasingly restrictive regulations. The landmark bill in Europe was the General Data Protection Regulation (GDPR) of 2018, which introduced strong protections in regard to processing personal data. The California Consumer Privacy Act (CCPA) introduced similar privacy requirements in the United States, with a compliance deadline occurring in January 2020. The overall momentum is to give more transparency and control to customers regarding their own data.

More than ever, organizations have to be smart about the information they collect. That means asking customers for permission and providing clarity about what information is being collected, where it's being stored, and how it's being used. Furthermore, customers should be able to access that information, and if they wish, they should have the ability to delete it. What companies were able to do with customer information five years ago is no longer possible, so leaders have to be more mindful and very intentional about the data they collect and their reasons for collecting it.

The limitations are only going to get more intense. For example, Apple is making changes to the Intelligent Tracking Prevention (ITP) feature on its Safari browser that will further restrict the use of tracking cookies. This, in turn, will make it harder to gain clarity on how customers use your website by limiting your ability to tie their sessions together in your data. Other browser owners are following and even going further. Google's stated intent for Chrome is to eliminate third-party cookies in fewer than two years.

In other words, you won't be able to unify the actions of an individual customer across multiple interactions with your media. "This consumer clicked an ad on this media channel, then later clicked another ad on this other media channel, then they visited our website." The days of that kind of attribution are coming to an end.

This doesn't mean you can't still do marketing analysis. It just means you have to do it differently. From a business standpoint, companies that embrace the change and become more mindful and respectful of customer data and use it the right way will inspire greater trust and appreciation, and customers are more likely to buy from a company they trust.

BUILDING IN-HOUSE DIGITAL CAPABILITIES

For a long time, it was common for companies, particularly large enterprises, to hire an agency of record (AOR), an outside company that was responsible for brand strategy and traditional media placement. The agency of record was also typically responsible for data analytics. However, in the last few years, many organizations have stopped hiring outside agencies and begun building their own in-house teams to handle the same tasks.

According to *Forrester*, 64 percent of companies now have in-house agencies, a dizzying 52 percent increase since 2008. Seventy-five percent of those in-house agencies have grown in staff size over the last two years, and over half employ fifty-plus full-time employees.[4]

There are multiple reasons for this trend, but we'll focus on two: a desire to take back ownership of their own data, and

---

4   Jay Pattisall, "Rethink The In-House Agency Hype," *Forrester*, November 13, 2018, https://go.forrester. com/blogs/rethink-the-in-house-agency-hype/.

improved agility. Brands often face many challenges in regard to transparency and a lack of direct control of their own customer data, specifically:

- Agencies often resist sharing data with other agencies, especially those that are perceived as competitive threats.
- Barriers come up when large agencies of record are asked to share data with smaller companies they perceive to be less qualified in the space.
- Brands often receive "top-level reports" on campaign performance without being given direct access to their own data for analysis.

These are just a few of the frustrations that organizations experience, but until recently, these frustrations alone haven't been enough for leaders to consider taking on the ownership and management responsibilities of in-house data. In reality, what has tipped the balance are the new customer data governance laws that we discussed earlier. Organizations are losing control of their customer data governance while still being held responsible for it, which has encouraged leaders to begin asking if they should manage all of their data directly.

Another reason organizations are creating their own in-house teams is because they provide greater agility. Rather than having to wait for an outside agency to respond to any changes in market conditions, decisions can be made and implemented quickly by in-house teams. They also provide an improved workflow. As Debbie Morrison, Managing Director of Ebiquity Group, said in *Marketing Week*, "It's the old chestnut around agility. To get a more agile route to market, brands are doing it themselves.[5]"

---

5   "UK Advertisers are Moving Marketing Services In-House," *Marketing Week*, March 21, 2017, https://www. marketingweek.com/2017/03/21/advertisers-marketing-services-house/.

DEFINING "IN-HOUSE"

When we refer to *in-house*, we're not talking about bringing video production, content marketing, creative strategy, or social media into corporate brand teams, though some have done that. Rather, we're saying it has become more common for brands to take direct ownership of all customer and campaign-related data in-house, bypassing their agency for collection, management, storage, and analysis.

The main benefits of this include greater transparency, real-time access to data, a gain of institutional knowledge, marketing agility, and end-to-end control, which help ensure compliance with the new regulations.

THE CHALLENGES WITH BRINGING DATA IN-HOUSE

On paper, bringing data in-house might look simple. After all, you already know which data you've asked your digital marketing agency to collect on your behalf, and you most likely know who the numerous vendors who touch that data are. Now, however, comes the more difficult part of data migration.

Do you have the right team? Do you have the right know-how? How do you plan to get your team up to speed, ready to take on the full responsibility of in-house data? Let's answer these questions.

Challenge #1: Acquiring the Right Team

It's a lot harder to acquire the right team than it might seem. Even if you make the business case and get budget approval to hire ten people to take on this effort, you're bound to encounter a few major hurdles. First, you will find that large companies like Google and Facebook are paying top dollar for the kinds of people you want to hire. Despite the research you did to figure out the compensation needs for each role on the team, your costs of acquisition are going to be higher than you expect.

The financial challenge is just the beginning. Once you interview interested candidates, you're bound to experience a bit of culture shock. Specifically, certain team members you want to add won't fit the culture of your company. Maybe they don't want to wear button-up dress shirts and slacks to work, or maybe they would rather work downtown than in the suburbs where rent is cheaper. Maybe they are chiefly interested in how fast they can get promoted, so they want assurance that they will get promoted within the next eighteen months.

Challenge #2: Having the Right Know-How for Getting Your Team Up to Speed

Even if you have a solid onboarding plan in place, you still need the right business know-how, and your team needs direction and guidance. Often, when an organization lacks specific skills, they will either hire new people or upskill existing team members, but if the team lacks a centralized focus, team members end up doing their own thing. The person responsible for marketing looks only at acquisition data, while the person responsible for CRM looks only at CRM data, and a third person focuses primarily on data visualization. Although each person might be a technical subject matter expert, the team ends up moving slower than ever because they lack unity about what they should be doing with their digital analytics.

When building an in-house team, you can bring a bunch of experienced people into your organization, a lot of high-quality talent, but you also have to provide clear direction to each of these individuals, so the whole team is unified and working together.

Challenge #3: Deeper Data Governance and Legal Ramifications

Perhaps the most difficult challenge to overcome when bringing data in-house is the need to create and enforce your own customer data governance policies. It's now your responsibility to avoid data breaches and prepare for all legal ramifications.

Prior to Europe's General Data Protection Regulation and the California Consumer Privacy Act, the biggest threat companies had to watch out for was data hacks. That threat has only gotten bigger as hackers have gotten more sophisticated, but there are now regulators seeking to ensure compliance with newly passed data laws. No one wants those regulators to make an example of their company.

THE HYBRID MODEL

Should you stay with your digital marketing agency, or should you go in-house with your data? There are big advantages and disadvantages either way. Fortunately, there's also a third option: the hybrid model. In the hybrid model, you hire a transition team to oversee your migration from agency to in-house, tasking them with ensuring a successful pass of the baton. Agencies and vendors can then play an ongoing role as you see fit. Just be wise in determining what you want to do in-house and where you prefer a partner's help.

At the same time, you partner with experts who help you map

out precisely what you need based on your strategy framework. With the right partners and the right knowledge, you can ensure a smooth transition while getting your new team established and ready to assume control of your systems and processes.

No matter which way you decide to go, you need to take a good, hard look at how you're going to handle your data with increased competition and changing legislation. The strategy that got you where you are today is unlikely to support your long-term growth ambitions.

Of course, world events might ultimately influence your decision about using an in-house agency. Since we started working on this book in the summer of 2019, many things have changed. Right now, as we said earlier, the entire world is in a state of emergency due to the COVID-19 pandemic.

By the time this book comes out, we hope the virus is behind us, and the world is recovering. However, it is hard to predict at this point how the economic fallout might impact in-housing. One theory says that enterprises will want to avoid adding to payroll, which will cause the in-housing trend to slow down or reverse. The opposite might also take place, with an increase in the perceived value of in-housing, such as agility and reduction in total cost. We can't say for sure how this will unfold, but one thing is clear: recovering from COVID-19 will require all hands on deck, and agencies will be pushed even harder to demonstrate and prove the value and ROI of their services.

ATTRIBUTION/MEDIA MIX MODELING

Attribution in the digital world can come in many forms, but the best definition for attribution is, "The practice advertisers use to give appropriate credit to every impression, interaction, or click that helps drive a conversion in a campaign." In other words, attribution is a process for giving credit to all of the online and offline marketing activities you are running to get your customers to recognize your brand and do something you want them to do on your digital platforms.

Today's shoppers see hundreds of different signals and messages from the advertisers and brands they're interested in, both online (through searching, social media, and email marketing) as well as offline (through television, billboards, in-store placements, word of mouth, and so on). There are hundreds of ways consumers can get exposed to the various brands, products, and services they engage with.

In light of customer data governance changes, organizations will have to focus more on *media mix modeling*, in which markets measure the impact of various media investments to determine how specific elements are contributing to sales conversions. Furthermore, this will become more of a *correlative analysis* than an aggregation because individual attribution will no longer be available.

In the section for attribution, we will take a deeper look into what attribution means for companies today, how to use it in relation to digital measurement, and the changing landscape as we look ahead.

CLOUD FOR MARKETING

There's a battle taking place in the cloud. Seattle is now becoming a cloud city as Google just announced opening a new campus, comprised of two blocks with 607,000 square feet of office space and 149 apartments, across the street from Amazon's cloud team.[6]

Microsoft, Amazon, and Google, among others, are all offering cloud storage. One of the applications of cloud is using customer data to optimize marketing. Google calls this application C4M *Cloud for Marketing*. The idea is to put all of your customer data on a single platform so you can tie it together into a unified dataset that ideally allows for a remarkable amount of analysis.

Recent buzzwords like "customer data platform" and "single customer view" are all related to Cloud for Marketing, as they are all powered by this concept. The real value and use case behind Cloud for Marketing comes from being able to take your various data sources and information about your customers and marketing activities, blend them together in an automated way, and glean new insights that would not have been possible when the data was siloed. The ability to activate this data from the cloud by building more advanced audiences off the merged data and targeting back into advertising channels is where the real magic—and high monetary returns—happens.

Of course, creating a unified dataset that integrates *everything* is a lot more difficult than it sounds. Though it has become easier, it still takes a huge amount of time and effort. However, even before all of your data has been brought together, you can benefit from the integration of multiple data sources. Working with multiple unified sources allows for more effective marketing *right now*.

---

6   Nat Levy, "Google Will Open New Seattle Campus This Summer, Just across the Street from Amazon's Headquarters," March 21, 2019, https://www.geekwire.com/2019/google-will-open-new-seattle-campus-summer-just-across-street-amazons-headquarters/.

Despite this, many marketers are waiting. "We need to bring in more data before we take action," they say. "We don't have everything yet."

Don't wait.

The beauty of Google Cloud for Marketing suite of solutions is that it allows you to use data to deliver advertising that is timelier, more relevant, and more personalized for your target audience. You don't have to wait for the perfect dataset. Instead, you can start using your integrated dataset immediately to make incremental improvements, even as you continue to build it.

GAINING CLARITY

As you can see, we are in the midst of many changes in regard to digital marketing, and the full implications of some of these changes haven't even been felt yet. Regardless of where you are in your organizational maturity, the landscape is certainly more challenging than ever. If you're falling behind in marketing analytics, it won't be easy to catch up, but don't panic. Once you gain clarity on where you stand as a company, you can begin to create a path for where you need to be.

In the next chapter, we will provide a framework that allows you to do just that. We want to help you get very specific about your *why*. That, in turn, will help you focus your analytics efforts to make some quick wins and build momentum toward the next stage of your organization's maturity. We'll help you put together a concrete plan that you can implement—no matter what stage of maturity you are currently at.

CHAPTER TWO

WHERE SHOULD YOU START?

CHAPTER CONTRIBUTOR: BRAD PRENGER

 Brad is a VP of Partnerships at InfoTrust. He is a driven and incredibly passionate brand and retail consultant with over fourteen years of experience in the digital media, e-commerce, and analytics industries. He strives each day to exceed goals, build partnerships, and showcase value with some of the largest organizations in the world. He provides a well-rounded perspective across media and analytics when talking with brands about their challenges in the marketplace. Brad's passion for building partner relationships and driving results is highly infectious, and he aims to bring value and success to InfoTrust for years to come.

When Brad isn't building partnerships, he spends time with his wife and three kids (two, five, and seven years old). Brad and his family live in Cincinnati and enjoy all things outdoors.

Which practices help companies run smarter marketing campaigns that will ultimately grow their business? What is the actual value of improving analytics capabilities? These are the central questions because right now, the marketing industry offers countless resources and platforms. It can be nigh impossible to figure out how to invest your marketing money wisely. The impact of any particular investment seems unclear.

To help companies take concrete steps in their digital maturity, Google commissioned Boston Consulting Group to create the *Mastering Digital Marketing Maturity* research.[7] In this research, they identified four stages of digital maturity. Briefly, they are:

- **Nascent.** A nascent organization is very media-focused, with a "campaign by campaign" level of thinking: "We need to grow our business. Let's run a YouTube ad." At this stage, companies mainly use external data and one-to-one buys. Since they often lack a full picture of their analytics data, they tend to think in isolated terms. They don't have enterprise analytics, so they just run individual campaigns to reach target numbers they've set, such as cost per click.
- **Emerging.** In the emerging phase, companies are beginning to think less about solving all of their problems through media and more about analytics tools. They've started using their own data instead of relying fully on media partners. With their own data, they are beginning to automate some of their marketing processes, using specific audiences and remarketing to combine media with tech stacks like Google Analytics 360 or Adobe Analytics. These platforms are allowing them to reach targeted audiences more efficiently

7   "Delivering Meaningful Moments," Google Marketing Platform, accessed December 28, 2020, https://
     marketingplatform.google.com/about/resources/bcg-delivering-meaningful-moments/.

and effectively. The company is beginning to understand analytics, combining third-party data with first-party data.

- **Connected.** This stage represents a big leap for an organization. They have finally begun to focus on and integrate data, bringing together all of the various data silos, such as marketing, analytics, and CRM, to drive ROI from a single customer point of view. This single customer point of view allows them to create more personalized campaigns as the company begins connecting the dots to create a solid digital analytics foundation. Nevertheless, many connected companies continue to think on a quarter-by-quarter or campaign-level basis. This short-term thinking creates an ongoing hindrance.

- **Multi-Moment.** It's at the fourth and final stage of maturity that a company truly becomes an analytics machine. Customer Lifetime Value (CLV) is taken into consideration when segmenting and targeting customers, so marketing decisions are optimized and personalized at a one-to-one level. A multi-moment company has data scientists combing through millions of customer records, putting them into different cohorts, then migrating that data back into an enterprise analytics stack, which enables the organization to buy media targeted differently toward high-value, medium-value, and low-value customers. As it turns out, the top 10 to 20 percent of customers drive most of the value for an organization, so a multi-moment enterprise spends a lot more on those customers.[8] They are able to do this because they have a clear, well-rounded, end-to-end understanding of who those customers are and the lifetime value they bring to the company.

---

8   Dave Lavinsky, "Pareto Principle: How to Use It to Dramatically Grow Your Business," *Forbes*, January 20, 2014, https://www.forbes.com/sites/davelavinsky/2014/01/20/pareto-principle-how-to-use-it-to-dramatically-grow-your-business/#2a88077e3901.

NASCENT

We "use" analytics on a very basic level, our data quality is questionable, and our team has a limited view on what is actually driving our performance.

EMERGING

We understand the importance of analytics to our business but currently relying heavily on third-party data. Our analysis and reporting is very siloed.

CONNECTED

We have a single POV of our customer; this allows us to understand media effectiveness and develop personalized campaigns, but we're still evaluating on a campaign level.

MULTI-MOMENT

We're an analytics machine with media being optimized by individual outcomes or transactions, using BigQuery for predictive modeling, revenue forecasting, and CLV.

© InfoTrust

A NEW FRAMEWORK FOR MATURITY: THE 6 PS

Everyone wants to jump immediately from nascent to multi-moment, but again, optimizing your marketing analytics is a *journey*. Sometimes, you have to crawl or walk, making consistent improvements over a long period of time before you can run.

When new partners come to InfoTrust for help, particularly large multinational corporations, they're often under pressure and have a long list of objectives. "We need you to fix our analytics. Then we need you to help us fix our media. Then we need you to help us fix our marketing stack so we can improve our marketing activities. And we need you to do it all fast!" They might list thirty-seven different objectives, and then they ask for a price quote, but they expect all of these things to get fixed within a couple of months.

However, as we studied this journey, we realized that moving from one maturity stage to the next requires some specific components to fall into place. Boston Consulting Group has done an excellent job of defining each stage, but we needed a mechanism to help people move from one stage to the next. So, we decided to make a framework of our own. Think of it this way: BCG gives you the treasure map, but you still need the right ship, crew, and resources to follow the map to the treasure. We built a vehicle to do just that.

We call it the 6 Ps of Digital Analytics Transformation.

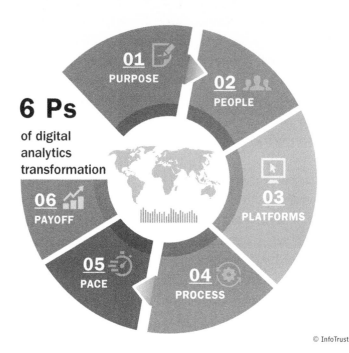

© InfoTrust

Maybe you're spending a lot on digital marketing and not getting results. Maybe you're struggling to understand the wants and needs of your high-value customers. Or maybe you're just looking to improve marketing.

Where do you start?

Simple. You start with purpose.

START WITH PURPOSE

Why do you want to become a better marketer? More specifically, in what *way* do you want to become a better marketer?

A few years ago, Facebook acquired Instagram, and then they acquired WhatsApp. In both instances, new tools allowed them to fulfill specific marketing needs. Founder and CEO Mark Zuckerberg had a vision for the company to become entirely mobile-focused, providing an amazing mobile experience. Data had revealed that more and more of his customers were moving in that direction, and so, with a specific purpose in mind, the company acquired the right tools and began delivering that experience.

If you lack a clear purpose, you will simply begin acquiring tools without optimizing them, creating a kind of Frankenstein monster that doesn't do much to deliver a better customer experience. At every stage prior to multi-moment, companies tend to be obsessed with simply acquiring and integrating more tools and platforms, but first, they need to start honing in on their *why*. Their purpose needs to become intuitive.

- Who is their customer?

- What does the customer expect from them?
- How can analytics help them deliver on those expectations?

PEOPLE, PLATFORMS, AND PROCESS

Once you understand your purpose, you can move from *why* to *how*. There are three basic levers of execution: *people, platforms, and process*. First, let's look at *people*. Even the best platforms need knowledgeable people to use them effectively, so upscaling your education and building the right team is the best investment your organization can make.

Avinash Kaushik, bestselling author and digital marketing evangelist, famously said that 90 percent of your budget should be used on people and only 10 percent on solutions.[9] In most organizations, these numbers are reversed. It's so easy to buy a new platform, and the number of options out there is breathtaking. All of these products promise better targeting, better cohort analysis, and so much more, but if you don't have the right people using those products, you're throwing money away.

It is *very easy* to fail on the people side of your organization. On your team, you need a business architect who understands how to use your analytics products effectively, and you also need a technical architect who understands how data flows between your platforms. This powerful combination ensures you get the most out of your products while also avoiding manual inefficiencies. You might be attracted to the shiny new analytics tool, but you need people who are dedicated to any tool you implement in your organization. Someone has to own it internally, or you won't get enough value out of it.

---

9   Avinash Kaushik, "The 10/90 Rule for Magnificent Web Analytics Success," *Occam's Razor*, May 19, 2006, https://www.kaushik.net/avinash/the-10-90-rule-for-magnificent-web-analytics-success/.

With the right people in place, you then need to select the right *platforms*. Much of Boston Consulting Group's framework focuses on integrating platforms for an important reason: you don't want to have a bunch of different analytics tools simply lying around. Learning how to integrate them effectively is the heart of maturity.

Not only do processes around marketing analytics and data flow become exceedingly easier when tools are automatically integrated within a simple platform, but the people within your organization will be empowered to collaborate and share ideas under the common toolkit. Siloed ownership and protectiveness around technologies becomes less of an issue as the common platform allows fewer comparisons and more action.

A single platform of integrated tools brings the promise of easier, faster access to actionable data that disparate product stacks lacking integration do not allow. The Google Marketing Platform is designed for this type of efficiency and enablement, particularly in activating your digital analytics data. We will discuss this more in the upcoming sections.

Remember, your platforms deliver or facilitate the *customer analytics value chain*. How efficient is the flow of data? If you have a lot of friction and drop-offs along the way, the data you're collecting about your customers might not end up in your data warehouse. If the flow of data is manual, not automated, you probably have a lot of inefficiencies, which can be very expensive, particularly for a large organization.

Once you have the right people and platforms in place, you are more than halfway there. Now, you need to put the right *processes* in place. Is your team using your platforms in a way that provides the highest ROI?

Usually, when we speak to companies about processes, they provide some kind of amazing flowchart they've developed over the course of a few months that shows what happens at each step. While flowcharts are a good start, they don't do much if the people within the organization don't understand exactly what their responsibilities are within the flowchart.

Maybe you have a social media marketer who comes in at 9 a.m.

- What are her specific analytics responsibilities while she's there?
- What sets of reports should she be looking at?
- What dashboards should she check?

Too many organizations lack good answers to these kinds of specific questions. For all the complexity of the process flow-chart, individuals within the organization have a muddled understanding of what they're supposed to be doing. You need to establish clear *marketing routines*. Remember, people tend to fall to the level of their training, so if you simply buy some fancy platforms and expect your team to rise to the occasion, you're bound to be massively disappointed.

Getting your people, platforms, and processes in place might seem like a tall order, but you need to think in terms of incremental improvements. Often, a new CMO will come in and start some big, ambitious project, but by the time they leave the company, the project is only halfway to completion. Another CMO then comes in, has no interest in the big project, and moves in a completely different direction. We know of companies that have been stuck in this cycle for *decades*.

Instead of planning a massive multi-year improvement project, concentrate on consistent incremental improvements to your people, platforms, and processes. This keeps the company moving forward, even as team members come and go over time.

What additional incremental revenue can you achieve by building or integrating new platforms, upscaling your people, and implementing daily routines? Maybe you're going to become more efficient with your advertising spending, or maybe you're going to become smarter about who, how, and where you target potential customers. In either of these ways, you can generate more revenue by simply reallocating rather than increasing your digital spend while also reducing ad waste. Gradually, your organization will become more profitable because you are making smarter marketing decisions.

However, you should also consider the capacity of your people. What is their capacity to execute? In many organizations today, capacity has been heavily impacted by recent events, with more people working from home, many people furloughed, and teams being reduced in size. Before upskilling your people, consider how much more they can handle. After all, if they're already deeply stressed, getting them to the next stage of digital analytics maturity is going to be more challenging, and it might be too much at this point.

If they don't have the capacity, can you afford to augment the team? Can you afford to either hire new people or work with a partner? If not, perhaps you will need to conduct a slow rollout or pivot your plans. Too often, organizations embrace extremely ambitious goals and assume that they simply need the right processes for getting there. However, if you don't plan for the capacity of your team, you might not be able to reach your goals.

PACE AND PAYOFF

The *pace* at which you implement these changes matters. How fast can your organization realize the value of your new solutions and platforms? In a sense, the pace is the clock speed of your business. How fast can you act on the data that you've collected? The answer to that question is going to be largely the result of how effectively the previous four components—purpose, people, processes, and platforms—are working. A slow pace is often the result of an unclear purpose, people who are not a good fit, weak processes, or platforms that are too basic.

There's also the pace at which you can recoup your investment. When an organization invests money into digital analytics—getting more people, buying new solutions and new platforms—it's important to consider how fast they can get ROI on all of that investment. You may need to prioritize projects that will help you get ROI faster, especially in our current environment, where many companies aren't even sure they will be in business by the end of 2021. Rather than just selecting the ultimate platform that you want to build in the next three years, consider what you can deploy now that will bring ROI in the next thirty to sixty days.

Then again, you might have amazing people and great platforms but still move at a snail's pace simply because you're in the crawling stage. As we said, you have to learn to crawl before you can learn to walk, and you have to learn to walk before you can run. When you can get all four (purpose, people, processes, and platforms) working seamlessly, your digital organization will be able to take advantage of the opportunities as they arise.

In terms of *payoff*, it's always best to have payoff goals that are well-defined at the beginning of any project. After all, the payoff is ultimately the indicator of success. It means your company is growing, learning, disrupting, and expanding. Generally speaking, there are two payoffs that you want to achieve as your organization matures. First, you want your marketing to generate more revenue, and second, you want to gradually increase the pace at which you implement new initiatives.

NAVIGATING THE STAGES OF ANALYTICS MATURITY

Let's take a look at each of the stages of maturity and examine what it will take for your organization to move from nascent to emerging to connected to multi-moment. As we move through the stages, we will pay particular attention to the 6 Ps.

NASCENT STAGE: BUILDING A FOUNDATION

At the nascent stage, you're not yet able to generate revenue as a result of analytics. You might not be clear on how analytics can drive value for your company, so you're not yet sure of what you should be spending on it. Maybe you've been burned in the past by spending money on fancy dashboards that never turned into revenue.

To determine if a company is in the nascent stage, we ask a question: "Are you now generating 10 percent more revenue as a result of analytics?" If they say no, or if they can't even answer the question, that's a big indicator that they are nascent.

When you are in the nascent stage, no one at any level of your company understands the value of analytics, and maybe they don't even trust the data. At the very least, you lack proper implementation, so you don't have insight into how your customers come to your website or their path to purchase. You might know that January was a great month, February was just okay, and March was amazing, but you're not sure why.

MATURING BEYOND NASCENT

The key to maturing beyond the nascent stage is to build an analytics foundation. Before you can build that foundation by implementing tactical analytics, you have to develop a strategy. What are the prioritized activities in which you want to drive efficiencies through marketing? How do you intend to more effectively reach your customers? What will be your key business drivers?

These questions help you create a strategy, and once your strategy is in place, you can begin to translate your business goals into analytics architecture for all of your websites, apps, and platforms. Your purpose at this point is to get a sense of the customer journey. How are customers coming to you, and what brings them to the point of purchase? Which platforms or marketing partners are actually driving your business? An infrastructure of analytics will begin to make this clear.

Once you have analytics architecture in place, you can begin developing processes in your organization to ensure that you consistently use analytics to move toward your goals. What is your process for adding new platforms or tags? What is the process for tag management? These processes keep your analytics ecosystem clean and consistent. Document them thoroughly. Too often, we see companies implement great processes, but they fail to document them. Six months after implementation, a new team comes in, and the processes are lost.

Finally, once you have a strategy, architecture, and processes in place, you're ready for platform migration. What platforms do you need, and what data needs to migrate to better understand your first-party data? You probably need to create a solutions design document, so your web developers can make necessary back-end changes to your website code to optimize your chosen platforms.

CASE STUDY: AUTOMATION

One of our partners just happens to be one of the fastest-growing fitness centers in the US. When they came to us, they were dealing with a pretty big operational challenge. They needed to deploy a new analytics solution to all 1,700 of their landing pages and micro-sites, but their website experience was highly fragmented. Each region had its own analytics setup, and some were better than others.

For an organization of that size, we recognized the need to automate their processes, enabling them to deploy things like GTM (Google Tag Manager) containers, properties, and marketing tags in a matter of minutes.

Previously, they'd only been able to implement these things by sending emails to individual location managers, who then implemented them piecemeal, which usually took hours, if not days, with multiple people working on them at each location. Automation helped them standardize their processes across the entire company, which freed them up to concentrate on activities that drove more revenue.

EMERGING STAGE: SILO THINKING

You can tell you're growing out of the nascent stage into the emerging stage when you start getting comfortable with your first-party data, even if you're still relying heavily on third parties for most of your marketing decisions. If those third-party companies shut down tomorrow, would you still be in big trouble, even though you're using more first-party data than ever? This is a hallmark of the emerging stage.

As an emerging company, you are still focused largely on marketing metrics such as CPM (cost per thousand), which measures the price of 1,000 impressions per webpage. Though you are beginning to connect some of your traditional marketing campaigns with analytics, you lack the integration to make one-to-one marketing decisions aimed differently at high-value, medium-value, and low-value customers.

Significantly, in the emerging stage, analytics is not yet customer-centric. Instead, you focus on individual channels: How are Facebook ads performing? How is Instagram performing? How is our website performing? What about our app?

If someone were to ask your company leaders, "How is your marketing performing overall?" they would have a hard time answering without resorting to channel-specific metrics. "We're generating a lot of leads on Facebook. Instagram is not doing as well." They haven't yet fully connected the dots across all platforms to create a holistic picture of their customers.

Measuring per platform creates a dangerous situation in which different teams or even individuals in the company have different ideas about how the company is doing. This becomes vastly more complex in a multi-brand CPG company because each platform has a different view of the company's performance for each brand.

"Our Facebook and Instagram campaigns are performing very well for this brand, but revenue is down overall. We can't figure it out!"

CONNECTING THE DOTS

To grow beyond the emerging stage, you have to start connecting the dots between your platforms, brands, and marketing, creating consistency in your analytics at a global level. You have to move from being channel-centric to being customer-centric. Your emerging company might have gotten really good at measuring individual markets or channels, but you need to start seeing the overall impact of marketing analytics on sales.

Silo-level thinking is rampant at this stage, so teams are each doing their own thing. The marketing team, analytics team, and governance team don't talk to each other enough, if they talk at all, so they lack a full end-to-end view of the customer journey.

In the nascent stage, you set your strategy, laid a foundation, and put your processes in place. Now, it's time to bring all of that data together holistically. As part of that growth, you also have to start thinking about customer data governance in light of the growing number of laws and data regulations around the globe, such as GDPR and CCPA.

Customer data governance becomes a big deal at this point in your maturity, especially with direct-to-consumer brands. As you move from third-party to first-party data, building your own analytics database, you have to start taking responsibility for that data. Are you giving customers the opportunity to opt out, to have their data returned to them or deleted? This is a necessary part of connecting the dots.

PLATFORM INTEGRATION

Ultimately, the goal of analytics is to understand your customers so you can drive the most value and create the best experience. We've seen situations where a marketing team will run an innovative, targeted campaign. It reaches people in Times Squares twelve hours before the ball drops on New Year's Eve, hitting all of the major media channels. Tons of people see it, but then, in the aftermath, the company doesn't have any idea of what the campaign did for them in terms of real numbers. In the follow-up, they couldn't tell you how many people came into their business, bought their product, or signed up for their newsletter as a result.

This problem frequently occurs in the emerging stage because marketing and analytics work in silos. It's time to bring them together. Marketing should ask, "When we run this campaign, how many incremental users will it bring us? What will the incremental revenue be?" The analytics team can then measure the campaign and provide the answers. Start scheduling regular joint meetings between your marketing and analytics teams.

You can run the coolest, flashiest ad campaign in the world and still lose market share to your competitors. We've seen it happen to many companies. If you want to drive more effective marketing that will, in turn, drive more profitability and better customer experiences, marketing and analytics have to work closely together.

CREATING VISUALIZATIONS

Having the analytics data is one thing; presenting it to people who might not understand analytics is another. Emerging companies have to start creating more visualizations and dashboards that communicate the meaning of analytics data to all stakeholders. Even those stakeholders who don't speak the language of analytics need to understand what is working and what isn't so they can make decisions accordingly.

Your visualization or dashboard doesn't have to include thousands of metrics. It doesn't have to look amazing. It just has to present the metrics that matter most to your business in a way that communicates their meaning to all of your departments and leaders. Ideally, any stakeholder should be able to derive meaning from the dashboard without having to learn all of the technical ins and outs.

With this simplified view of the data, you are selling the value of your platforms and integrations and providing an accessible way for leaders and teams to make decisions based on relevant metrics.

GROWING PAINS

In the emerging phase, companies tend to go on a hiring spree. As they acquire new capabilities in-house, they need qualified people to make the most of them. The danger is that they over-hire, or they hire too quickly without having a clear idea of how to structure their teams.

This is also the maturity stage when companies begin playing with the idea of building a data warehouse, pulling all of their data from multiple sources into a single place, and putting customer data governance into place. It's still a product-centric organization, but an evolution begins to take place. They're moving in the right direction, and every part of the organization begins demanding analytics. There's more call for reports and dashboards.

Along with an increased interest in analytics comes a whole slew of problems, as multiple teams and individuals throughout the organization start to use different products and channels. There is a danger of duplicating their efforts. There's also the danger that people will start doing too much.

It's like when you first sign up for a fitness club, and you set an aggressive workout schedule: "On Sunday, I'll run. On Monday, I'll swim. On Tuesday, I'll lift weights. On Thursday, I'll fast. On Friday, I'll play tennis. On Saturday, I'll do aerobics." Initially, you might feel amazing, but eventually, you're going to get burned out. You'll be so tired, you'll start to lag in every area. It's not the best way to achieve your fitness goals. It would be far more effective to create a single integrated fitness plan and work out less often with a more unified purpose.

As your people get excited about the possibilities of analytics and begin implementing it throughout your organization, there will come a time when you need to do some correction. The excitement is great, but it can turn into panic. To stave that off, you'll have to bring some activities in line, unifying your focus, so you keep moving in the right direction.

CASE STUDY: EMERGING INSIGHTS

A partner of ours, one of the largest B2B e-commerce companies in the world, implemented a product carousel on their cart page. A product carousel offers recommendations to customers about additional products they might consider adding to their cart. Everyone in the organization thought it was a good idea. How could it not drive more sales?

Since the company was entering the emerging stage, they decided to test their idea with analytics data, so they put their A/B testing platform to good use. Integration at this stage took a lot more work than they expected, but once it was done, they were able to collect data about the impact of the product carousel on customer behavior.

To their surprise, they found that it actually deterred customers from completing purchases. The list of additional products became a distraction. When they removed the carousel from the cart page, they experienced a significant increase in revenue.

These are the kinds of insights you start to gain in the emerging stage. Decisions are starting to get confirmed or corrected with actual data, and analytics starts to make an impact on revenue, even if there's still a lot of work to be done to become truly customer-centric.

CONNECTED STAGE: AN INTEGRATED VIEW

In the emerging stage, you're bringing in platforms and upscaling your people with real analytics data, but many decisions remain isolated, and silos still exist. You reach the connected stage once you finally bring all of your efforts together to create a single customer view.

You're not marketing one-to-one yet, but you understand different audiences and cohorts. You've brought together numerous platforms and integrations, and with them, you now have a holistic view of your customer. This, in turn, drives more effective media and greater profitability.

Your customer relationship management (CRM) is integrated within analytics, so you now have confidence that your data is correct. Everyone in your organization believes in the data, and you've begun creating a true data warehouse. Though your data warehouse may still be somewhat isolated from your decision-making, from an analytics standpoint, all of your platforms and teams work together like a well-oiled machine.

You're no longer making marketing decisions for specific channels: "What do we do for Facebook? What do we do for Instagram? What do we do for our website? What do we do for our app?" Now, you can see your customer across all of these channels, so you know how each specific channel plays into the broader picture of customer behavior.

CONNECTION QUALITY

When you've connected all of your data, some of that data might be flawed. Some companies get hindered here because they think all of the data has to be perfect before they can start making decisions.

Fortunately, this is not the case. The process of integration takes a long time to perfect, and even if some of the data coming in isn't accurate, you still make better decisions. Honestly, there's no such thing as perfect data because customer behavior is never perfect. Ideally, you improve the quality of your data over time, but you can start making connected decisions now.

Some aspects of connecting data become more difficult at this stage, particularly in regard to customer data. As we've said before, we may be slowly entering a cookieless world, so your ability to overlap customer data, tying interactions across multiple platforms to a single person, could become almost impossible.

Even without regulations, connecting data from a variety of channels is no easy task. So many third-party companies create flashy new platforms that claim to connect everything in one amazing dashboard without any need for integrations. These are empty claims. There is no single tool that can make you a connected organization overnight. It takes time, and it requires integrations.

To get there, you have to understand each platform and how it connects with other platforms, which is complicated. That's why there are data engineers. Facebook, Google, and Twitter aren't hopping on the phone with each other to say, "Hey, how can we work better together?" On the contrary, they are directly competing with each other in the media space. All the hard work of connecting them to create a holistic customer view falls on the companies that use them.

AREAS OF FOCUS

There are a few primary areas where your organization should focus its effort in the connected stage in order to reach the multi-moment stage. We recommend that you focus on advanced integrations, real-time dashboards, and data-driven attribution.

ADVANCED INTEGRATIONS

In the emerging stage, you start making basic integrations between marketing and analytics using an enterprise tool like Analytics 360, but in the connected stage, you begin to integrate your in-house or third-party CRM (e.g., Salesforce™) with both analytics and offline data. That offline data might include sales you make through a third-party retail store.

With advanced integrations, you no longer have siloed data sources. Instead, you bring everything together into your data management platform to gain a picture of the customer journey from start to finish. This includes more than just what customers do on your website or within your media campaign. If you have fifteen different ways that customers connect with your company, all of those touchpoints must become connected into one overall view.

REAL-TIME DASHBOARD

At the connected stage, you must be able to make decisions quickly, so you need real-time dashboards where you can see the data. If it's a key time frame, such as Black Friday, you need to be able to see the data midday, so you can make adjustments on the fly to hit your daily goals.

In the emerging stage, companies often work quarter to quarter. "We ran this test last quarter, so we now know what worked and what didn't. Let's make some changes for the next quarter." In the connected stage, you should be able to make many same-day decisions, seeing real-time revenue by platform. You should know at any particular moment what is driving performance and what isn't.

DATA-DRIVEN ATTRIBUTION

In working with global organizations, our team has observed a pattern across media campaigns. For example, a company will run a large campaign that results in broad exposure, then look at the data and say, "We spent $10 million on this campaign, and it didn't work." Suddenly, everyone in the organization—including investors—hates both the campaign and the media platform used.

Google Display Network is the most common media platform used for these campaigns, and so many organizations have a love/hate relationship with it for this very reason. However, it's a mistake to think of the platform as a direct contributor to the last customer click.

At the connected stage, you have to move past a platform-centric mindset that says, "This platform drove X amount of sales." Instead, start to see the entire customer journey and identify the steps that drive the most revenue per customer. For example, "A customer first sees our ad on TV. Then they search for us on Google or Bing and get a display ad. Then they click on the ad and go to our website."

Data-driven attribution allows you to identify the best combination of touchpoints in the customer's journey. Maybe Display doesn't generate any direct sales, but data reveals that it plays a role in the overall customer journey for a significant number of customers. In that case, it still deserves credit as an important touchpoint.

It's not, "How many sales did Display generate?" It's, "Did our combination of TV, search, Display, social media, and email drive customers down the funnel fastest for maximum profitability?"

We talked in much greater detail about attribution in chapter seven, so refer back to that chapter for more specific information about the role it plays in digital analytics.

CASE STUDY: QUICK DECISION-MAKING

One of our partners is a high-end beauty retailer, and 60 to 80 percent of their revenue comes from specific seasonal time frames. A high sales season can make or break them for the year. They have to win during those time frames, and the beauty industry is a highly competitive space.

Utilizing Google BigQuery, we built an intraday revenue and conversion forecasting model for them that fed their marketing and media decisions on an hourly basis. The company created an entire "war room" dedicated to this dashboard so that, on an hour-by-hour basis, they could see where they stood in relation to their projected end-of-day revenue. This allowed them to make quick decisions, adjusting tactics and spending throughout the day. It worked so well that they've scaled it across all of their consumer brands and retail shops.

Of course, this kind of dashboard only works when your data sources are connected. Otherwise, you end up predicting for each channel and making a dozen or more different predictions, none of which provides an overview. Your ability to predict outcomes works a lot better when you've tied together multiple data sources.

MULTI-MOMENT STAGE: A WELL-OILED MACHINE

By the time you reach the multi-moment maturity stage, you have become a well-oiled analytics machine. You're ahead of the curve at all times—a best-in-class marketer. At this stage, you have connections between the cloud, your analytics, your marketing, and your CRM. Everything is integrated on a one-to-one basis. You can predict what a customer is going to spend in the next three, six, nine, and twelve months. You know who your best customers are going to be and which customers are likely to churn. Predictive modeling is firmly in place, and you make decisions around customer lifetime value.

You have integrations with a cloud instance. A cloud instance is a virtual server that allows you to bring together all of the data from different parts of your organization, including first-party and third-party data, online and offline data. In essence, it creates a shared pool of resources that can be easily accessed.

Multi-moment organizations take advantage of technology and complex features, so you have also begun to embrace advanced cloud features such as machine learning, sentiment analysis, and facial recognition tools. For example, maybe you're a real estate company, and you're using machine learning to evaluate properties.

The multi-moment stage is about more than marketing analytics. Your internal operations have become more effective and efficient because you know your customers. You use predictive modeling and forecasting to inform you about how many products to produce so there is minimal discrepancy between what's sitting on the shelf and what is leaving the shelf. You can predict retailer demands, so you know in advance what's going to be a hot product in the coming months.

In the multi-moment stage, you understand product correlation and basket analysis, so, for example, you understand that a particular skin care product sells well with a certain eye care product. You know that if you place those two products close together on the webpage or on the shelf, it will drive more purchases. This might even influence the way you package the product because you know which types of packaging are more profitable.

Marketing doesn't necessarily become easier at this stage, but you learn faster because of your predictive models and because you can interpret the data more clearly now. Even if something doesn't generate ROI, your teams see it as a learning opportunity, with lessons to be applied to future efforts. Ultimately, you are focused on long-term success and profitability.

Every data source you have is automated, actionable, and purposeful. Your teams don't have to waste days putting together reports because your reports are automated. The information is already available. All you have to do is interpret the data so you can spend more time on the business side of analytics.

A word of warning! Just because you reach the multi-moment stage doesn't mean you'll stay there. You can always fall out of this stage, so make sure everyone in your organization, from top to bottom, has fully bought in. Make sure teams continue to innovate, evolve, and test.

THE MOST IMPORTANT METRIC

We've partnered with companies that had over five million individual customers in their customer relationship management (CRM) system with ten years' worth of data, and we had to help them mine all of that data within a cloud instance so they could start making sense of it. It is always a monumental task. With that data, their data scientists have to determine, first, which of those five million customers are active. Then they have to predict what their sales to each of those customers will be over their lifetime—the all-important CLV.

Customer lifetime value is the heart of multi-moment maturity. When you can take a granular look at customers and make marketing decisions based on forecasted revenue, then you can really hone your efforts and your spending. In an increasingly competitive world, this is the key to analytics maturity.

ALIGNING THE TWO FRAMEWORKS

The real power of digital marketing maturity comes from aligning the Boston Consulting Group's four stages of maturity with our framework, the 6 Ps of Digital Analytics Transformation. The 6 Ps are the specific components you have to work with as you move toward analytics maturity. We've grouped them into three sections. First: *why* you need to do this (purpose). Second: *how* you accomplish it (people, platforms, process). Third: *how* you measure the success of your work and demonstrate it to management and your executive team (pace, payoff).

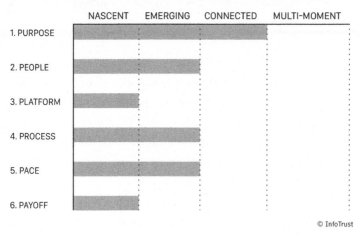

Combining the Analytics Maturity Framework with the 6 Ps of Digital Transformation (Sample results shown)

	NASCENT	EMERGING	CONNECTED	MULTI-MOMENT
1. PURPOSE				
2. PEOPLE				
3. PLATFORM				
4. PROCESS				
5. PACE				
6. PAYOFF				

© InfoTrust

IT'S TIME FOR A SELF-ASSESSMENT

The frameworks we've provided are key to your digital transformation, but to make use of them, you need to know where your organization currently stands. Taking an honest look at yourself isn't always easy, and in our experience, companies tend to be too hard on themselves. We've seen organizations of all sizes, from Fortune 500 companies to small businesses, who are doing at least a few things exceptionally well. They need to improve other things, but that's just the nature of business. You're not going to be excellent at everything, nor should you expect to be.

Ultimately, you need to know your organization and have a clear sense of your core competencies. After all, if you want to become a *Harvard Business Review* case study, all you have to do is become consistently good at a few things, but that means you're also going to have hundreds of projects that are probably not particularly successful. As long as you are learning and refining your efforts and making incremental improvements, you are moving in the right direction. Don't be too hard on yourself. Just be honest, learn from the things that don't work, and keep improving.

Woody Allen famously said that 80 percent of success is showing up. We think he might've been speaking about marketers. The biggest part of effective marketing comes from simply being consistent with your efforts, improving them as you go. Now, of course, if you keep doing something that doesn't work, that's the definition of insanity. Learn what works, improve, and keep at it. That's what it comes down to.

We've created an assessment you can take to evaluate where your company currently sits so you can determine where you need to go. Beyond identifying your maturity stage, we want to help you see those key areas of improvement. Have you defined your purpose? How are you doing in terms of people, platforms, and processes? Do you need to change your pace? Are you generating payoff from your marketing activities?

Maybe you've already reached the multi-moment stage of maturity. First of all, if that's the case, give us a call. We would love to hear your story. Second, and more importantly, how can you sustain your competitive advantage? Even the most mature companies are at risk.

Since 2000, 52 percent of companies in the Fortune 500 have either gone bankrupt, been acquired, or ceased to exist.[10] Think of the cautionary tales like Sears. Sears dominated the retail

---

10 "Digital Transformation Is Racing Ahead and No Industry Is Immune," *Harvard Business Review*, July 19, 2017, https://hbr.org/sponsored/2017/07/digital-transformation-is-racing-ahead-and-no-industry-is-immune-2.

industry for decades, but in recent years they've experienced a shocking decline.

Building momentum is important, but maintaining that momentum is an ongoing challenge. How can you continue to innovate? How can you constantly upscale your people? No matter how mature your company is now, you still have to reinvest in people and platforms and optimize processes.

On the other hand, maybe you are just getting started. Maybe you launched a new company that is just beginning to navigate the nascent stage. There is so much potential revenue in your future if you can begin to move the needle.

Wherever you are, there is work to be done, and there are improvements to be made. We want to help you on that journey.

To better help you understand where you are in the analytics journey, we have compiled an assessment on the following pages. To access a digital version of this assessment and complete it online, visit infotrust.com/crawl-walk-run/.

DIGITAL MATURITY SELF-ASSESSMENT

Digital Maturity Self-Assessment

WHAT IS THE PURPOSE OF YOU COLLECTING CONSUMER/CUSTOMER DATA?	
Choose One	**Why?**
A	Digital Maturity Self-Assessment	
B	Gain Consumer Insights	
C	Provide Great Consumer Experiences	
D	Enable Retargeting	
E	Get Better at Testing and Optimization	
F	Delivering Great Marketing ROI	
G	Unknown at This Time	
H	This Has Not Been Finalized/Approved/Confirmed by Management	
I	Survive the Pressure of Our Competitors	
J	Other Purpose (Please Fill Below)	

_____

_____

_____

_____

_____

_____

PEOPLE (Team = In-House, Outsourced or Hybrid)	0	1	2	3	4	5	People Sub-Score
1	Does your team do advanced analytics like CLV?							
2	Do you have a dedicated team with clear accountability?							
3	Do you measure team upskilling?							
4	Does your team understand the importance of first-party data?							Add all of the scores from this section below
5	Does your team understand the value of Customer Analytics?							
6	Do all the platforms in your stack have an owner who is responsible for them?							
7	Does each person/team have clear objectives and success metrics?							
8	Do you have at least one team member that knows how all Customer data flows through your entire ecosystem?							
9	Does your team know how to use Customer data as a competitive advantage?							

PROCESSES	0	1	2	3	4	5	Processes Sub-Score
1	Do you "own" your own data? Specifically, can any employee or third party you wish have access to it?							
2	Does your team do digital marketing with excellence across all digital touchpoints?							
3	Do you have a process to address all upcoming data privacy regulations such as CCPA and GDPR?							
4	Are analytics processes turned into clear marketing routines that people execute every day?							
5	Do you rely mostly on first-party data to drive marketing and sales?							Add all of the scores from this section below
6	Do you have clearly defined KPIs for each of your customer touchpoints?							
7	What percentage of reporting and measurement tasks is automated vs. done manually by your team?							
8	Do you measure the effectiveness of your analytics?							
9	Are you able to drive financial results/gains from your investment in analytics?							
10	As your analytics improve, is the ROI on your investment in Analytics improving?							

© InfoTrust

PLATFORMS	0	1	2	3	4	5	Platforms Sub-Score
1 Do you have an analytics platform?							
2 Is your Customer data integrated and activated across channels with a demonstrated link to ROI or sales proxies?							
3 Do you have a CRM Database that everyone who needs to can access it?							
4 How fragmented are your CRM tools?							
5 Are most/all of your Platforms connected such that Customer Data easily and consistently flows through your enterprise?							Add all of the scores from this section below
6 Does your team know the reason for each of the Customer Platforms in your ecosystem?							
7 Is there a structured process for how new platforms are selected and adopted?							
8 Do you have a data governance platform?							
9 Is the ROI of your analytics platforms measured?							
10 For each new platform that you add, do you know the incremental gains via known KPIs that you can achieve?							

PACE AND PAYOFF	0	1	2	3	4	5	Platforms Sub-Score
1 Are you able to measure the impact of analytics on your business?							
2 Have you seen improvements of key metrics, such as COA, conversion rate, ROAS, etc.?							
3 Have you been able to recoup your investment made into your digital stack?							Add all of the scores from this section below
4 Are you able to execute your advertising campaigns more quickly than you were prior to investing in improving your analytics maturity?							
5 Has investment in platform automation and integration removed manual work and inefficiencies?							

DIGITIAL MATURITY TOTAL SELF-ASSESSMENT SCORE:

WHERE ARE YOU ON YOUR JOURNEY?	NASCENT	EMERGING	CONNECTED	MULTI-MOMENT
	0-50	51-100	101-150	151+

Plot Your Score

PART TWO

• • • •

DEEP DIVE

Ensuring that your organization is able to progress through the digital analytics maturity journey while building a solid purpose with the right people, platforms, and processes to drive pace and payoff will set your organization up for success. While we recommend a "crawl, walk, run" mentality with your digital analytics activities—learn to crawl before trying to walk, and learn to walk before trying to run—it's good to have a clear sense up front of everything you need to consider.

In our work with more than forty Fortune 500 companies, we've discovered a few key areas where your organization can focus on driving both quick wins and long-term success. We will dive into those areas in this next section of the book, but bear in mind, the topics we're about to cover are incredibly complex. If you're not already well-informed, they might seem overwhelming at first. However, they are going to make a profound impact on your marketing, operations, and technology stack.

We want to help you take a step back, gain an understanding of these vital topics, and get clarity on how they impact your digital growth strategy. We will show you how they contribute to your ability to provide an unmatched customer experience, making it easier for consumers to decide to buy and continue to buy from you. After all, data analytics ultimately comes down to understanding and delivering on customer expectations. If you can't do that, nothing else matters.

In the next section, we are going to discuss customer data governance, Google Marketing Platform, Google Analytics 4, Attribution, and Cloud Platform. You may wonder why we cover data governance first, particularly in a book about data analytics. The truth is, data governance is the foundation of everything your organization should be doing when collecting online data about customers. It will be a heavier, more in-depth chapter, but this is intentional. There are so many ramifications when it comes to customer data governance. If you're a marketer, it is important to familiarize yourself with the concept so you can share the specifics on compliance with your legal team. Your organization needs to work on becoming compliant with all of the regulations that are being enacted.

While the information we share on this topic should not be interpreted as legal advice, it can still serve as a handy resource for the changing data governance landscape. After all, if you get your customer data governance wrong, nothing else that you do with data analytics matters. Bear in mind, data governance regulations vary from country to country, even state to state, so it is a highly complex issue. For that reason, we will also point you to some additional resources to bring you up to speed.

After customer data governance, we will discuss Google Marketing Platform, which incorporates all of the solutions an organization needs to collect data and analyze its advertising campaigns. Then we will look at Google Analytics 4, which enable you to unify your measurement of user interactions between your app and websites. Finally, we will look at Cloud for Marketing, where an organization can begin to combine its data with other datasets for more advanced use cases. Bear in mind, none of these resources can be implemented without the right people and processes, so we will consider the 6 Ps as we look at each one.

Let's begin with customer data governance.

CHAPTER THREE

CUSTOMER DATA GOVERNANCE

CHAPTER CONTRIBUTORS:
KENT OLDHAM AND LUCAS LONG

 Kent Oldham retired from Procter & Gamble after thirty years as an executive. During his last five years with the company, he led privacy and security work across more than a thousand customer-facing websites. In his role as Head of Customer Data Governance at InfoTrust, he is a trusted advisor to our global multi-brand clients. As a husband and father of three boys, Kent enjoys what his family enjoys.

 Lucas Long is a Senior Tag Governance Specialist and Tag Inspector™ Product Manager at Info-Trust, working with global organizations at the intersection of privacy regulations and technical tag management. Through these efforts, he helps global organizations across verticals ensure complete and compliant data collection. When not discussing the intricacies of GDPR,

CCPA, and cookie laws with clients, Lucas enjoys traveling and exploring new cultures, one bite at a time.

We invited Kent and Lucas to coauthor this chapter in order to share some of their wisdom and insights from delivering global customer data governance solutions to the largest enterprises in the world.

Customer data governance is foundational to any successful digital maturity journey. Though it is generally related to the crawl phase, companies are picking up the pace on this topic given the current privacy environment. The purpose and eventual payoff of customer data governance are to create trust with customers while deriving value from the data they entrust to your organization.

Disclaimer: The information in this chapter is not intended to be legal advice or counsel and is not represented as such by InfoTrust or Tag Inspector. We do not make any warranties or statements regarding the legal acceptability of the information presented in this workshop. Actions performed as a result of the information provided are of your/your company's own choosing. Please obtain legal advice from legal counsel whenever taking action related to the law.

In this deep dive, we will focus specifically on the people, processes, and platforms that contribute to successful data governance. Let's begin by clarifying our terminology. What exactly *is* data governance?

To put it simply, data governance is the capability that enables a corporation to maintain high-quality data throughout the life cycle of that data. In this chapter, we will focus exclusively on customer data since it is, by far, your most valuable data. In today's world, as regulations tighten, you have to be extremely careful with your customer data. In such an environment, how can you continue to provide the most value to your customer base?

THE RISE OF PRIVACY REGULATIONS

In recent years, we have seen an increase in privacy regulations due to certain companies abusing the rights of customers and doing whatever they wanted with customer data. With the passage of the General Data Protection Regulation (GDPR) in the European Union in 2016, the regulatory environment entered a new, more intense, and more difficult era for marketers. In the immediate aftermath of its passage, but before the GDPR went into effect in 2018, organizations had numerous questions and concerns, both about the nature of the new regulation and the way it would be enforced.

Fines for violating the new rules are not handed out by the EU as a single governing body but by individual national governments, adding further to the complexity and uncertainty. In terms of actual numbers, the maximum fine that can be levied against an organization for misuse of customer data is 4 percent of its gross revenue. That means a company with $1.25 billion in revenue could be fined as much as $50 million.

That's not something any organization can shrug off. A large, multinational corporation could easily wind up with total fines in the billions of dollars. This possibility has stoked a fire, spreading fear throughout many industries.

California passed similar privacy regulations in 2019 with the

California Consumer Privacy Act (CCPA), which went into effect in January 2020. Like the GDPR, the CCPA was driven by a desire to protect consumers. With CCPA, there are two tiers of fines: $2,500 per violation for an unintentional violation and $7,500 per violation for an intentional violation. As you might imagine, this can add up quickly. If you run an e-commerce site with 10,000 visitors, a single, unintentional violation becomes a possible fine of $2,500 × 10,000. Suddenly, a single mistake costs you $25 million. Ouch!

And the regulatory parade continues. As of 2020, at least twenty-five states in the US have either passed or have introduced consumer privacy regulations.[11] This number is only growing. For an updated list of state legislations similar to CCPA, visit iapp.org/resources/article/state-comparison-table/. Also, be sure to visit infotrust.com/crawl-walk-run/ for additional ePrivacy resources.) From an IT standpoint, staying compliant is becoming an increasingly ominous task. To deal with all of these state regulations, many companies have begun pleading with the federal government to step in. Heavy but unified federal regulations seem preferable to death by a thousand paper cuts!

The essence of these regulations is that companies must inform customers about what will be done with their data. That's why when you visit many websites these days, you get a pop-up banner that says something like, "We use cookies. Are you okay with us collecting your information? Please, refer to our privacy policy." California adds a new twist in which customers must be able to opt out of companies *selling* their data. Furthermore, companies can't penalize a customer for opting out.

---

11   Michael Beckerman, "Americans Will Pay a Price for State Privacy Laws," *The New York Times*, October 14, 2019, https://www.nytimes.com/2019/10/14/opinion/state-privacy-laws.html.

The real challenge of the California regulation comes into play when a customer makes a request concerning their data that a company is in possession of. If a customer contacts a company, providing their email, phone number, or other information, within forty-five days of receiving that information, the company must reconnect with the customer and inform them of what categories of data they've captured and what precisely has been done with it.

This is easier said than done. After all, tracking the flow of an individual's information through tags and pixels becomes extremely difficult as that information flows throughout an organization's many data systems.

The scope of what companies are accountable for goes well beyond interactions visitors have with a digital asset to include any and all customer systems of record like CRM (customer relationship management) databases, data lakes, and any other database or tools containing consumer information.

By law in California, customers have a right to know about all of it. To comply, you need a clear understanding of the customer data being held throughout your organization, and then you must be able to retrieve that data and provide it to the customer—in plain language, not in some cryptic form. Last but not least, a customer can ask a company to delete all of their data, and the company is required to do so within forty-five days. This is called *right to erasure*.

Consider the consumer data you have collected. Do you actually know where all of this data is located in your organization? Do you know what categories each piece of data falls into? Can you provide that data back to customers in an efficient manner? Finally, can you then delete that data if a customer requests it?

If your answer to any of these questions is *no* or *I'm not sure,* you have work to do to meet regulatory demands. Of course, you may not do business in California nor meet the minimum thresholds for coverage under the law, in which case you are not subject to CCPA. However, the rise of privacy regulations means that no matter where you do business, similar regulations are bound to impact you sooner or later. For this reason, you need to *immediately* start creating a customer data governance strategy to get your data under control.

CREATING A CUSTOMER DATA GOVERNANCE STRATEGY

Tracking customers has become far more difficult as privacy regulations increase. Getting in on the act, tech companies like Apple and Google are changing how they manage the life span of cookies. For example, first-party cookies often expire within twenty-four hours now. As a result, a returning visitor to your website looks like a new visitor. The challenge is this: given the regulatory and technical restrictions, how can an organization meet the spirit of customer privacy requirements while also providing targeted marketing capabilities?

Obtaining customer insights and getting the most out of your media spend is harder than ever. What does this mean for you? It means cookies, tags, and third-party data are going to become less prevalent. Going forward, your strategy needs to leverage first-party data more than ever.

Unfortunately, for many companies, a customer data governance strategy is an afterthought. Mostly, they just want to avoid getting sued or fined. After that, they might try to figure out what they can do with the remnants of their data. Given the privacy restrictions in place, competitive advantage is not just realized by who can best analyze and action their data but by those who can collect the most in a compliant manner.

Embrace this change and enter the new increased privacy future boldly!

WHY ARE YOU COLLECTING CUSTOMER DATA?

The first step in creating your customer data governance strategy is to determine what customer data you need and why. We're amazed at the number of people we speak to who can't articulate a purpose for collecting customer information. "We collect data because we know it is valuable," they say.

Once you can define the *purpose*, you can begin to strategize *how* you're going to acquire vital first-party data. In terms of the people who need to be involved in this process, we recommend including not just digital marketing and digital analytics but also your lawyers. They're the ones who will help you interpret relevant laws and regulations, while the analytics team helps with execution.

Ideally, the people involved in data governance need to be a cross-functional team with input from marketing, legal, security, performance, and analytics. Beginning with the purpose, the strategy is going to be defined by the marketing team; advertising and communication needs inform what data is collected, the platforms necessary to drive initiatives, and how the data will be used. Once these aspects are defined, the organization can then break down the specific data points being collected and processed for these purposes and work with legal to determine any privacy or regulatory restrictions that must be adhered to.

For regulatory requirements, disclosure to users is important, giving users the ability to opt out or restrict processing, as well as providing the mechanisms to respond to access requests from users. Security needs to be involved to make sure proper protection and technical architecture are in place. Finally, performance must be considered since these platforms will be implemented across digital properties and factor into the overall user experience and site architecture. Having inputs from all of these relevant business units is critical to defining, implementing, and maintaining an optimal data governance program within your organization.

CREATING VALUE FOR YOUR CUSTOMERS

The second step in creating your customer data governance strategy is determining the value you will provide to customers in exchange for their data. How will you convince consumers to trust you so they are both willing and happy to provide you with their information?

The burden is on you. Your job is to understand your consumer deeply enough that you can provide them with a simple and transparent reason to trust you with their information. The difficulty of obtaining first-party data varies depending on your business, but, no matter what, you're going to have to provide some kind of perceived value to consumers in order to convince them to gladly share their information.

This could be something as simple as fun quizzes or games on your social media, or it could be vital information, interesting videos, free trials, discounts—the possibilities are endless. Remember, only collect what you need. Do not collect for the sake of collecting. Your trust is on the line.

WHERE IS YOUR DATA?

The third part of your customer data governance strategy is to make sure you have control of the valuable customer data you have been entrusted with. Start by asking simple questions like: Do you know what customer data you have? Do you know where it is located across your entire ecosystem? Do you understand how it flows through your ecosystem while maintaining its integrity? If you answered *no* to any of these questions, it is time for an audit.

An audit is important to establish a baseline of what you know, what you don't know, and how you can *get to know what you do not know*. Armed with this knowledge, you can create your tag governance policy and practices.

WHAT ARE TAGS?

A tag is a piece of JavaScript code running on a web page that has a number of specific functions. Tags collect data points from users, browsers, and web pages, sending that information to corresponding analytics or advertising platforms. Tags also set cookies to store information observed from the user. These cookies can then be accessed later to connect a series of interactions for individual users across multiple web pages or websites. Tags are often tied to some front-end functionality, such as social media posts on Facebook or LinkedIn, acting as your initial point of collection.

Tag Inspector, InfoTrust's proprietary tag auditing platform, features an extensive tag library of over 2,600 tags. To get a free, comprehensive audit of your tag architecture, visit taginspector.com/free-scan.

A few years after becoming a certified Google Analytics partner, we worked with a global multi-brand organization, helping them roll out Classic Analytics as a global solution, migrate to Google Analytics Premium, and move all tags to BrightTag.[12] This included migrating all analytics from the source of the pages into one central tag management system. A core challenge became verifying that all on-page code was removed and Google Analytics code was present and loaded through the tag management system on every page. There was no scalable way to programmatically audit tags across thousands of sites. In response, we created Tag Inspector.

Tag Inspector is a tag auditing and monitoring platform which gives organizations visibility into the digital marketing, analytics, and advertising platforms loading on each page of a site. It displays each tag that is present, how each platform loads, and the data collected by each one. Soon after launch, we realized the information surfaced by the tool had applications far beyond verification of analytics deployments. The reporting fills a massive need in giving organizations the visibility necessary to address data governance challenges.

Today, Tag Inspector is the tool of choice for enterprise organizations to audit the current data collection practices on their digital properties, guide them through tag governance policy creation, and monitor adherence to the policy in the live environment. It powers the data governance programs for hundreds of organizations globally and is even used "under the hood" for audit functionality within some of the most widely adopted tag management systems on the market.

---

12   BrightTag was the original name of the tag management system currently known as Signal, https://www. signal.co/.

Combining the insights gleaned from Tag Inspector with our expertise in analytics and data governance, we have defined the processes necessary to develop a comprehensive data governance program. Let's explore the steps in this process.

CREATING A TAG GOVERNANCE POLICY

This is a great place to pause and again visit infotrust.com/ crawl-walk-run/, where you can find many complementary and exclusive resources that will help you get the most out of this book. Now, on to tag governance policies.

Tag Governance Process

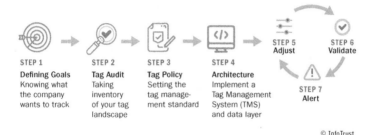

© InfoTrust

A comprehensive tag governance policy should include the following:

- A list of approved tags to be loaded onto your digital properties
- The specific data points collected by each tag
- The internal team and contact responsible for each platform
- The external teams associated with each platform
- Data sharing agreements associated with each platform
- An outline of requirements for compliance with any and all relevant privacy regulations

- Records of approval from legal, security, and performance teams
- The dates of implementation and scheduled dates for removal and review
- Documentation of all implementation and data-collection requirements from both the business and vendor

In addition to a formal policy and documentation, a defined tag governance process is also necessary. The process will include a few different layers:

- A new tag or vendor request and approval process
- A new tag implementation process
- A process for ongoing review

AUDITING PROCESS

Of course, to create a comprehensive tag governance policy, you first have to understand what you're already working with, so we recommend conducting an audit. To do that, we recommend using a tool like Tag Inspector (taginspector.com), which allows you to scan and identify all live platforms. For your initial report, it's good to start with a *tag inventory* (examples can be found at infotrust.com/crawl-walk-run).

With one view, you get a list of all of the live marketing, advertising, and analytics platforms loading on your website. You also have additional columns containing context for each platform, which includes the general category and subcategory to help you understand any unknown platforms, along with what we call the *initiating tag* containing the first two levels of load behavior. This context helps you understand if a tag is loading from the page via the tag management system (TMS) or if it's piggybacking off another third party that is implemented on your site.

From here, it is important to go through each platform and fill in the business context necessary for the governance policy. This business context includes the following:

- **Business Owner.** The team and specific internal contact who is responsible for "owning" the platform. This would likely be the individual who signed the agreement for the tool or the primary internal administrator utilizing the tool.
- **Agency Partner.** Often, media and marketing tags are requested and added to a website on behalf of an agency partner to run campaigns and provide reporting. If that is the case, indicate who the partner is and the primary contact at the organization. (Important note: Even if an agency partner has requested and "owns" the day to day of a platform, there should still be an internal owner responsible for governance and compliance. There's too much at stake in this new privacy environment for your organization not to maintain internal ownership of all platforms and tags.)
- **Legal Approval.** If a tag has been vetted and approved by your legal team, indicate that here. Also, aggregate any and all corresponding documentation, as you will need this for compliance and governance documentation.
- **Security Approval.** If a tag has been vetted and approved by security, indicate that here. As with legal documentation, include any information provided by the vendor as it relates to the security of data collected and processed. Again, you will need this for compliance and governance.
- **Performance Approval.** If a tag has been tested and approved by the team responsible for site performance, indicate that here. If there are any performance requirements, you will

want to state those in your governance policy as well. While this is not required for compliance purposes, many organizations have performance baselines that tags must adhere to.

- **Approval.** Indicate here if a tag is approved to load on the website. The prerequisite should be full vetting for privacy, security, performance, and that the tag is still being actively used by the business. On your initial audit, many tags will need further vetting before final approval is given. This column will be used as the basis for your approved list of vendors in your tag governance policy.

Your initial inventory of tags associated with your business will often uncover two things:

1. The presence of legacy tags that are no longer in use but still loading on your website.
2. Tags piggybacking off or loading through third parties that you weren't aware of.

In both of these scenarios, these tags can be indicated for removal, providing an easy win.

After your initial inventory and business context review, it is time to conduct an in-depth data review of all tags that have been tentatively approved to ensure compliance with relevant privacy legislation. For the purposes of this book, we have focused on Europe's GDPR and California's CCPA, but you need to audit your tags for all regulations relevant to your business. For each of these, you need to do a deep dive of the data collected by each tag. Again, using a tag auditing platform such as Tag Inspector, you should aggregate all parameters and values that each tag is sending to your respective platforms.

First, evaluate each tag, and ensure compliance with all relevant data-collection regulations, fully mapping out all data collected by each platform. By parsing all requests sent by the tags, you can begin to evaluate the data collected for governance purposes.

Here is an example of what an exported output might look like using Google Analytics tag requests:

PARAMETER COLLECTED	PARAMETER (TRANSLATED)	EXAMPLE PARAMETER VALUE
uid	User ID	abd0222184741
v	Protocol Version	1.2
t	Hit Type	Pageview
dl	Document Location	https://infotrust.com
ul	User Language	en-us
de	Document Encoding	utf-8
dt	Document Title	infotrust
sd	Screen Colors	24-bit
sr	Screen Resolution	2560x1440
vp	Viewport Size	2545x1225
je	Java Enabled	1
cid	Client ID	1314378.224

The key is to understand all the data points collected so you can evaluate if personal data (GDPR) or personal information (CCPA) is being collected and processed. If so, that platform will need to be considered for the processing, disclosure, and storage requirements as outlined in each of the regulations.

Let's walk through the full process of evaluation for GDPR and CCPA regulations.

GDPR GOVERNANCE ASSESSMENT

Using the data mapping explained above, fill in additional context about the data points collected by each platform. (Again, an example of what this might look like can be found on our website infotrust.com/crawl-walk-run.)

First, note if any of these data points can be considered personal data as defined by GDPR. If so, the following questions need to be answered:

- What is the purpose of the data being collected?
- How long is the data stored?
- What technical protections are in place to ensure the safety of the information?
- What operational protections are in place to ensure the safety of the information?

Knowing the answers to these questions will help with the necessary documentation for processing this data, and it will contribute to the full considerations necessary for GDPR. Once all data collected by each of the tags loading on your site have been evaluated, you can then aggregate the results and answer the core GDPR audit questions at a platform level.

- Is this tag or platform processing personal data?
- If so, what is the legal basis for processing it? For marketing, media, and analytics tags, this will either be "legitimate interest" or "consent."
  - If there is a legitimate interest, what is it?
  - If there is consent, is your consent mechanism GDPR-compliant? Are all platforms configured to only process personal data when consent is given? Does the user have the ability to remove consent?

- Are all necessary data sharing agreements and other contracts in place to ensure compliant sharing and access to data?
- Given the requirements of GDPR, is the platform properly reflected in your privacy notice?

We have created a helpful infographic specifically for the GDPR evaluation process of each platform. Check it out at taginspector. com/articles/infographic-gdpr-tag-audit-process/.

CCPA GOVERNANCE ASSESSMENT

Similar to the GDPR assessment, you need to follow the same process in evaluating the data being collected to make sure it meets CCPA requirements. Using our data mapping for each tag as the foundation, work through the relevant CCPA compliance questions for each data point.

With the CCPA assessment, you need to work through the following:

- **Personal Information**: Would the data point be considered personal information as defined by the law? If so, proceed to the next bullet points.
- **CCPA Category**: Within the CCPA text, there are a number of defined categories. The category of information is important for disclosure purposes. Assign each point of personal information a category as defined by the law.
- **Use Description**: This is a description of how the personal data is used.
- **Data Shared**: Indicate if the data is shared with any other parties, and if so, with whom?
- **Data Sold**: Indicate if the data is sold to any other parties, and if so, to whom?

Following this assessment of all data being collected by each tag on your digital properties, it is important to aggregate the data and ensure that proper disclosure is provided to users. If any of the data is being sold, the user must have the proper mechanism in place to opt out of the sale of that data. Make sure you have all necessary legal documentation and data sharing agreements in place for these purposes as well.

By now, you should have documentation created and aggregated for each platform as it relates to the main privacy regulations for digital properties. Following the GDPR and CCPA assessments—along with the business audit completed at the beginning of the audit process—you can *finally* aggregate the information and create your initial tag governance policy.

Organizing this documentation within your internal systems will ensure that all necessary information is at hand and that full evaluations can be completed to definitively say which platforms are allowed and included in your policy. All non-compliant tags, in addition to those determined to be not in use, should now be removed from your websites, giving you a clean and compliant foundation.

Once that is done, you need to ensure that you remain compliant moving forward.

ONGOING MANAGEMENT

Having a compliant website today is not enough. You will also need a compliant website tomorrow, next week, next month, and next year. Therefore, it's important to develop sound processes around tag governance.

Let's take a look at the three core processes necessary to ensure compliance.

1) NEW TAG/VENDOR APPROVAL PROCESS

This process should be undertaken whenever a new platform is requested to be added to your website. Collect all of the information that is necessary for review and approval by the various interested parties (legal, performance, security, etc.), as well as all information necessary for your tag governance policy. By requiring all of this information at the time of request, you ensure that policy documentation is kept up-to-date and all live platforms have the necessary information for future compliance reviews.

Information that should be requested includes:

- Tag/platform name
- Business owner (specific contact)
- Agency partner (if applicable)
- Start date of deployment
- End date of deployment
- Description of business use case
- Documentation about the platform being requested
- Data sharing agreement
- Specifics about the data being collected
- Specifics about the cookies being placed
- Documentation for relevant privacy regulations

The format for this documentation should be the same as the initial audit. It should be platform-specific and fed into your aggregate policy documentation, outlining compliance and business information at a high level.

2) TAG IMPLEMENTATION PROCESS

Following the formal review and request process, any new platforms that need to be added to the website should go through a formal implementation process. This process should be utilized not only by brand-new platforms but also previously approved platforms that are already included in the approved tag list that require new instances to be implemented for new campaigns, landing pages, or site instances.

A solid tag implementation process should be owned by a single, central team. The workflow will look like this:

1. A defined team first implements the tag in a staging or pre-production environment.
2. The implementation is reviewed by either an internal development team or a technical resource from the vendor in question.
3. The tag is verified to be behaving properly.
4. The configuration is published to production.
5. The live configuration is signed off on by the business team responsible for the tag, ensuring that the necessary data is flowing into reporting or that the necessary functionality is working as expected.

This process is often managed within an internal ticketing system so that records of progression through each stage can be recorded and made visible to all relevant parties. As long as all necessary information is submitted during the initial request process, the implementation team should have all of the technical documentation necessary to implement it.

In some cases, a new instance of a previously approved tag might have additional or custom requirements. As long as no new data points are being collected, these can go through as preapproved. However, if there are new data points or technical specifics being introduced, those should be vetted and added to the documentation of the platform in the overall tag governance policy.

3) PROCESS FOR REGULAR REVIEW

The final process is a regular review that ensures all live tags have been vetted and approved by all required stakeholders and that your website is maintaining compliance with applicable laws and regulations.

It is important to have a defined end date for all tags approved in the tag governance policy. Vendors often change their configurations and enhance the capabilities of their platforms. In the case of third-party tags, this means that the data being collected and how it is processed could change. To be proactive, all approved platforms should have an end date no longer than eighteen months following the date of deployment.

In the case of media tagging or analytics specific to campaigns being run, these platforms (or unique instances of the tags) should have an end date that corresponds with the date of completion of a campaign. Be sure to consider any attribution window following this end date as well. Using these end dates to trigger a new review of all approved tags will ensure that your organization stays on top of compliance necessities.

MONITORING AND MAINTENANCE

You have audited your platforms, you have created a tag governance policy, and you've created processes to ensure ongoing compliance. Now, it's time to institute ongoing monitoring as an alarm system to help identify any violations of approved tag behavior.

To do this, you'll want to use a tag auditing and monitoring platform. Again, we recommend Tag Inspector because it has functionality that allows you to input your tag governance policy requirements to create a *whitelist rule* that indicates the approved platforms defined in your tag governance policy. Apply this rule to regularly scheduled scan audits of your websites, so you are automatically alerted to any unauthorized tag behavior.

Since you're dealing with third-party JavaScript tags, the configurations that define the data being collected are maintained and updated on the vendor side. Ideally, you trust all of your vendors and should have legal documentation in place restricting their ability to collect new data points or use collected data in additional ways, but you still lack control of updates made on the vendor side.

It is always possible for an unauthorized data point to be collected or another third party to be embedded and begin loading on your site. Institute a monitoring process using a tool like Tag Inspector, so you're always alerted to such behavior. Use the guide we've provided above to simplify the process of auditing, maintaining, and monitoring your tag governance process. In doing so, you should be able to stay on top of your tag governance and avoid any unintended consequences or regulatory penalties.

Your Turn:

- Use this quick questionnaire to see where you are on your governance journey: infotrust.com/resource/customer-data-governance-self-assessment-checklist/.
- See what tags are loading on your site and how: taginspector.com/.
- See what an example output from an audit looks like: infotrust.com/crawl-walk-run.

CHAPTER FOUR

GOOGLE MARKETING PLATFORM

CHAPTER CONTRIBUTORS: AMIN SHAWKI, MELANIE BOWLES, AND ARIEL OPELT

 Amin Shawki is Head of Growth at InfoTrust. He has been with the company for eight years, leading hundreds of digital transformation projects with some of the largest e-commerce, CPG, multi-brand, and news and media organizations in the world. He has trained dozens of organizations across numerous verticals and regions, showing them how to activate their data, connect different systems, and build effective teams, processes, and platforms with Google Marketing Platform technology.

 Melanie Bowles has been in the digital space for over eight years, working on both the agency side and client side. She has been involved with the development of digital and optimization strategies for both SMBs and Fortune 500 companies across multiple industries. Specializing in digital transformation, Melanie has been a catalyst for helping businesses increase traffic, improve customer experience, and increase conversions and revenue. Melanie is currently an Optimization and Insights Specialist at InfoTrust where she partners with multifunctional teams to define analytics strategy, analyze data, and evaluate the business impact of digital experiences.

 Ariel Opelt is a Lead Digital Analytics Consultant at InfoTrust. In her role, she works with global brands to develop and implement global and local website tagging plans, provide advanced reporting, train in-house brand teams, and optimize audience targeting. Previously, Ariel worked as an in-house marketer covering areas such as organic search, paid search, and social and email. With her marketing background, she fully understands how data can be siloed and works with her clients to offer innovative solutions to overcome this barrier.

We invited Amin, Melanie, and Ariel to coauthor this chapter in order to share their experiences leveraging Google Marketing Platform across thousands of sites, including multibillion-dollar-per-year internet retailers and direct-to-consumer brands.

In this chapter, we will take a look at Google Marketing Platform (GMP), examine what it has to offer, explore how it can help your organization ascend through the analytics maturity framework, and discuss how it can enable you to put together a robust digital analytics set up.

Google Marketing Platform provides the tools you need to become a well-oiled analytics machine. Through its comprehensive suite of products, you can coordinate multiple teams, share data, and create a single customer view, all of which are vital to go from crawling all the way to running.

Google Marketing Platform is actually a suite of products and tools that provide numerous ways to improve your digital marketing and analytics. It has been designed with marketers in mind, so it is less complex and more seamlessly integrated than other analytics enterprise platforms. At InfoTrust, we've helped dozens of organizations deploy GMP products at various maturity stages.

Google Analytics has become the most popular free analytics tool in the world, and it forms the core of GMP. You may be asking, as many have before, why did Google create a unified platform rather than simply developing separate products? Digital marketing has become highly complex. There are thousands of ad and marketing tech products on the market that enable organizations to engage with customers, including ad-serving products, search management products, tag management, and on-site analytics. The ecosystem is very disparate.

With Google Search, Google Campaign Manager, Google Display & Video 360 (previously known as DoubleClick products), YouTube, and other video platforms, as well as products like Google Analytics and Google Tag Manager, Google saw the value in integrating these products closely with shared management to simplify enterprise usage. So, it created Google Marketing Platform to unify its key products, both from a capability perspective and overall management, helping marketers take their digital analytics and marketing to the next level.

By unifying all of these products under a single platform, it brought together best-in-class technology that allows seamless data sharing between products.

Google Marketing Platform also allows centralized management, which makes it easier for organizations to make data-driven decisions, and it provides advanced features like audience targeting without the need for a lot of overhead or custom solutions for data sharing. After all, when you try to connect different vendor platforms to share data, you can experience data loss, and it takes a lot of work to maintain those integrations. With Google Marketing Platform, however, these integrations are built-in and fully supported by Google.

Though we are primarily talking about platforms and processes in this chapter, bear in mind that as your organization onboards more solutions, you will need to upscale your people in order to increase the capacity of your team.

Why Use Google Marketing Platform?

Best-in-class Technology at each stage of the programmatic ecosystem

Complete Data Fidelity means no data loss between your digital platforms

Advanced Feature and Audience Targeting through platform connections

Centralized Measurement for all media enables precise optimization & spend efficiencies

© InfoTrust

GOOGLE MARKETING PLATFORM PRODUCTS

As of August 2020, Google Marketing Platform includes seven products: Google Analytics, Google Data Studio, Google Optimize, Google Surveys, Google Tag Manager, Display & Video 360, and Search Ads 360 ("360" signifies a solution is paid and designed for enterprise use). Google Analytics, Optimize, Surveys, and Google Tag Manager all have free and 360 versions available. Additionally, two other products worth mentioning are Campaign Manager and Google Studio, which Google has stated will be a part of the Display & Video 360 product. By bringing them all together, Google Marketing Platform creates a seamless integration of data sharing, so your digital marketing team, product team, and business decision-makers can quickly access your data and share it among themselves.

There are many advantages in connecting these products, but the essence is better accessibility to data sharing, which makes it easier to gain visibility and activate audiences than ever before. This is more important than ever as the changing governance landscape and privacy laws continue to restrict customer data.

Of course, Google offers numerous other products to help with your marketing strategy, including BigQuery, Cloud products, Google Ads, and Google Firebase for mobile ads. While these products aren't technically part of the Google Marketing Platform package, they seamlessly integrate with GMP products as well.

What all of these GMP products have in common is that they offer enterprise-focused capabilities and licenses with either Google or a certified partner for additional benefits, such as SLAs (service level agreements), uptime of product, freshness of data, and guarantees of issue resolution.

Another question you may ask yourself is if you already have Google Analytics, does that mean you already have Google Marketing Platform? Technically, yes, because Google Analytics is one of the eight products that are part of GMP. Just by having the free version of Google Marketing Platform, you have access to an incredible amount of information and reports, though you lack a license agreement that gives you access to Analytics 360 or the other enterprise-level products. While you can get an individual license for Analytics 360, that doesn't include things like Campaign Manager and Optimize. Investing in Google Marketing Platform offers distinct advantages through the integrations of all GMP products.

The seven essential Google Marketing Platform products always operate as a single unit, which means, among other things, that changes made to Google Analytics are always made with the other products in mind. Product teams at Google don't work in silos, so they are able to create more intelligent tools and customizations to meet enterprise needs with a high degree of control. They provide the ability not just for data collection of digital assets (through Analytics 360 and Campaign Manager) and data visualization (through Data Studio), but also Ad Serving, Programmatic Advertising for Display, Video and Search, as well as on-site AdTech management (Google Tag Manager) and on-site testing and personalization (Optimize).

To summarize, the key advantages of Google Marketing Platform are integrations that provide a complete solution for digital analytics and marketing needs, a focus on enterprises that includes guarantees, SLAs, and support, advanced capabilities, such as attribution and predictive analysis, key features that aren't available on the free products, and, perhaps most importantly, built-in audience creation and sharing.

Of course, you can run these products separately if you wish. For example, you could invest in Campaign Manager and Display & Video 360 without using Google Analytics, but bringing them together allows a far more impressive amount of audience-building and customer engagement. The kinds of integrations provided by Google Marketing Platform help move your organization along the maturity framework.

A REVIEW OF GMP PRODUCTS

Let's take a look at each of the seven Google Marketing Platform products to gain a sense of what they offer individually.

GOOGLE ANALYTICS AND ANALYTICS 360

First, the core of GMP in terms of data collection is Google Analytics. The free version of Google Analytics can be deployed on any website, and you can create an account easily through Google.

However, the free version has some limitations that make upgrading to Analytics 360 enterprise edition well worth the investment. First, the free version includes a monthly hit limit. If you get a certain number of hits per month or per session, Google will limit or even cease collecting and processing them. This is called sampling: extracting only a subset of your total hits or sessions for your user interface.

Google Analytics vs. Google Analytics 360

	Google Analytics	Google Analytics 360
Target Audience	Individuals, small- and medium-sized companies	Large and/or Advanced Enterprises
Multiple data collection options across websites, apps, and internet-connected devices	✓	✓
Data access via mobile app, API, email notifications, and more	✓	✓
Advanced site and app reporting and segmentation (including real-time and user-centric reporting)	✓	✓
Native data integrations with...	Google Ads, AdSense, Ad Exchange and Search Console	Google Ads, AdSense, Ad Exchange, Search Console, DV 360, SA 360, Campaign Manager
Native remarketing integration with...	Google Ads	Google Ads & DV 360
Advanced analysis, integration with Google BigQuery, SalesForce	✗	✓
Funnel Reporting and Attribution Modeling (DDA)	✗	Advanced
Cross-property roll-up reporting, unlimited data, unsampled reporting, access to raw data	✗	✓
Number of views per property	Max 200	Max 400
Custom dimensions and metrics per property	20 custom dimensions	200 custom dimensions
Data Freshness	Not Guaranteed	Guaranteed 4 hours under SLA
User and account administration	✓	✓
Support and Services	Self-service help center and community forums	Service, suppport, and SLAs provided by Google and global partner network

© InfoTrust

Note: Google Analytics and Analytics 360 change over time, so the contents of this matrix may vary. Visit infotrust.com/crawl-walk-run for up-to-date feature comparisons.

The purpose of sampling is to make the processing and reporting of data extremely fast, and fast access to data allows data-driven marketing decisions. However, sampling can lead to inaccurate analyses because you lack a complete raw dataset. With Analytics 360, you have access to unsampled data so you can see all of the hits and raw data captured on your digital properties, and you have a much higher threshold in the user interface for how many sessions you can see before sampling occurs.

The free version of Google Analytics also has fewer reporting features, and data isn't as "fresh" in terms of how soon you will be able to report on the data captured from your digital assets. Analytics 360 refreshes data every four hours or less, as guaranteed by your service-level agreement.

With the free version, data is only refreshed and processed every twenty-four to forty-eight hours (though we have seen much faster processing speeds, it's not guaranteed). One clarification is that both Google Analytics and Analytics 360 enterprise version have real-time reports, but this is only for a limited subset of attributes and metrics that are captured and shared in the reporting user interface at the time the hits are collected.

The biggest difference between the free version of Google Analytics and the enterprise version is the amount of world-class support that's provided. The free version doesn't provide a way to contact a Google account representative for your organization directly, though there are chat features within the user interface for their general support and, of course, hundreds of public forums with information too. With the enterprise edition, you have dedicated resources for implementation assistance and ongoing technical support. You are provided an account representative you can speak to directly for help, customized training on a regular basis, access to new betas, and more.

CAMPAIGN MANAGER

Another key piece of the Google Marketing Platform is Campaign Manager (previously known as DoubleClick Campaign Manager), which is an ad-serving technology that gives marketers and advertisers tools for placing display ads and some social ads. It provides a single platform for centralizing, analyzing, and acting on a holistic view of the customer across all of your ad tech. You can manage duplicated activities, such as ads you want to push to multiple sources, and control the frequency of ads being shown to your customers. You can also optimize your media and look at the path to conversion.

DISPLAY & VIDEO 360

Display & Video 360 (previously known as DoubleClick Bid Manager) gives customers access to high-value display and video inventory, including numerous major publishers, such as ESPN. You can run ads on publisher websites to get in front of your customers and potential customers while they are navigating across the internet. You can also negotiate the cost of display ads for specific publisher websites directly within the Display & Video platform.

Display & Video 360's access to inventory and customers enables you to reach specific, targeted audiences, and there are many, many options for the types of customers you target based on their interests and the websites they visit. Plus, when you connect to other Google Marketing Platform products, such as Analytics 360, you can input first-party data and overlay it with third-party data.

The real value of Display & Video 360 is that Google's machine learning and high-powered automation drives the performance of your media buys and placements. You don't have to do all of the strategizing and bidding manually. Display & Video provides the information and even does some of the optimization, so your ads get in front of your customers at the right time.

SEARCH ADS 360

Search Ads 360 (previously known as DoubleClick Search) is a search aggregator tool that allows you to manage multiple search engines and search advertising in a single place. Instead of dealing separately with Google Ads, Microsoft Advertising, and Yahoo Gemini (now a part of Verizon Media Native), and other search engine platforms, you can centralize all of that management into Search Ads 360 and automate much of your search campaign management.

The ability to set up, optimize, manage, tweak, and edit search campaigns across all search engines at scale from the same platform is incredibly helpful for organizations with hundreds or thousands of keywords that they are trying to target on paid search. Since you can manage them at scale, it's perfect for enterprises with many products and many customers they want to reach.

Search Ads 360 also provides optimization tools, including automated bidding, budget management, structural changes, and even trigger-based changes to your campaigns in real time. Even better, Search Ads 360, Display & Video 360, and Campaign Manager data capture and tracking of conversions are all shared within Google Marketing Platform, creating unified reports without the need for deduplication manually.

This is all done through the shared conversion process and

single pixel known as Floodlight tags. Floodlight tags measure conversions and collect data about your site visitors to power audience creation and assess campaign performance. Depending on your Floodlight architecture, you will often have unique instances tied to specific campaigns. Auditing your website to ensure only necessary Floodlights are loading and collecting all necessary information is critical to optimize campaign and site performance.

Let's suppose a customer sees a video ad through Display & Video 360 and, separately, a paid search ad through Search Ads 360, and both of those ads contribute to conversion. By having these tools integrated, you prevent each platform from receiving a full conversion and thereby inflating the value of each. The Google Marketing Platform dedupes this behavior with Campaign Manager's Floodlight conversion pixel, and goes even further with Google Analytics conversion tracking for any source or medium, even outside these GMP, previously known as DoubleClick campaigns.

Types of Data Available by GMP Product

Google Ads	Google search engine ad data
Search Ads 360	Cross-search engine ad data
Campaign Manager	Cross-exchange display & Video ad data / All paid media
Analytics 360	Organic search & other Analytics 360 media / Website data

© InfoTrust

TAG MANAGER AND TAG MANAGER 360

Analytics 360, Campaign Manager, Display & Video 360, and

Search Ads 360 are tools designed for advertising within Google Marketing Platform. Google Analytics and Campaign Manager also provide plenty of reporting, data collection, seamless deployment of analytics, and optimization within our digital platforms. This is where Google Tag Manager and Google Tag Manager 360 begin to play a vital role.

Google Tag Manager is designed to help you manage your tags in the ad tech you've deployed on your website or mobile app. It provides a safe, reliable, and accurate way to deploy tags, so you have accurate data collection across all of your platforms for things like user engagement, interactions, and conversions. Google Tag Manager is easy to use and provides debugging platforms and error checking, so you can deploy your marketing ad technology much faster.

In the days before tag management tools, requests for website changes, such as adding analytics code or tracking snippets, had to go through IT and typically involved a long process. Google Tag Manager streamlines such efforts and provides more control, making it a critical piece of Google Marketing Platform.

DATA STUDIO

Data Studio is a product that allows you to connect all of your data sources, even Excel files, so you can build a dashboard and visualize your data easier. While there used to be a paid enterprise edition, it is now completely free.

As one of the fastest-growing Google products, Data Studio automatically plugs into Google Analytics and Campaign Manager, so you can create beautiful dashboards that are fast, easy to load, and automatically update as you collect more data within your platforms. The beauty of Data Studio is the prebuilt data connectors for both GMP products and non-Google vendor products, and new automated connectors are being built by the community all the time.

Consequently, if you have another customer data source that you want to include in Data Studio, you can either build an automatic Extract Transfer Load (ETL) process for it (which we discuss in the Cloud for Marketing chapter) or use one of the prebuilt native integrations provided by Google or one of its partners.

However, the single biggest advantage of using Data Studio instead of reporting directly from Google Analytics or Campaign Managers is that it offers a more simplified way to create beautiful, shareable dashboards. You can add or remove collaborators and build dashboards in real time.

During the first few months of the COVID-19 pandemic, we saw many organizations considering to begin leveraging Data Studio to cut costs. While it does not have all the bells and whistles that its competitors feature, it does address the most common data visualization needs. (Visit infotrust.com/do-more for more details on potential budget-friendly actions, such as switching to Data Studio.)

OPTIMIZE AND OPTIMIZE 360

Optimize is a website optimization and personalization tool in GMP that allows you to tailor your customer experiences to specific user segments. You can run A/B, multivariate, and redirect tests, and you can personalize your content using powerful targeting capabilities. Since Optimize is natively integrated with

Google Analytics, you can use your existing Google Analytics metrics and objectives to identify problem areas and turn those insights into action.

With Optimize, you can use the metrics already built into Google Analytics, such as transactions, revenue, and custom event tracking, as objectives for your tests with no additional setup. Native integration means any Google Analytics audiences you set up can be accessed directly for targeting purposes.

Optimize also offers native integration with Google Ads, allowing you to target users referred from specific Google Ads campaigns, ad groups, and even keywords. This integration means you can create customized landing pages based on specific user intent and interests to test the impact on your ROAS (return on ad spend).

OPTIMIZE VS. STANDALONE PRODUCTS

Optimize is part of Google Marketing Platform, but there are other experimentation tools offering similar solutions that are outside of GMP. Why should you choose Optimize instead of a standalone product?

The biggest advantage of Optimize is that you don't need to do any additional implementation on your site when setting up test objectives. Any goals or custom events you have set up in Google Analytics properties are automatically available for your experiments—a major time-saver. Most testing tools require additional coding on your site to collect the behavioral data necessary for measuring your test objectives and predicting outcomes. Optimize is the only experimentation tool that offers this type of native integration.

Optimize provides a number of basic targeting options, such as the ability to target users on specific devices and browsers or in certain geographic locations. However, you can also choose from a number of advanced targeting options for users coming from specific campaigns or who share a common attribute.

If you use Google Analytics, you're probably already familiar with UTM parameters, which track the effectiveness of online marketing campaigns across multiple sources. With Optimize, you can target users based on data layer variables, JavaScript variables, even first-party cookies for any advanced testing implementations you need to do.

OPTIMIZING YOUR AUDIENCES

Your audience strategy is key to your analytics maturity, and Optimize provides countless ways of targeting user groups. We recommend starting with low-hanging fruit in order to get some early wins. Begin by analyzing how users interact with your site on different devices—mobile, desktop, tablets, and so on.

Look at the way users coming from different ad campaigns interact with your website, then dial into specific user groups. You might find that certain users share common behaviors, allowing you to target them in specific ways. Using this audience strategy, you can customize content using personalization tools on Optimize to streamline experiences for your users.

Run A/B tests and deploy customizations based on your findings. If you run a test for three different user groups, you can determine how each group is most inclined to convert. Deploy variations for each group through Optimize.

OPTIMIZING YOUR TESTING PROCESS

We love the intuitive interface provided by Optimize. It is visually appealing and easy to understand, which makes scanning your results for variants and probabilities much simpler than with most standalone products. You don't need a statistician to understand the results.

Optimize's personalization features are robust. Almost anything you can run as a test can then be deployed as a personalization. The idea is to discover what is relevant to the interests of your visitors and run website experiments to see how they respond. You can then create and deliver personalized experiences to promote greater engagement. This works well with paid search, particularly Google Ads, which is integrated with Optimize, so you can run personalization based on the keywords that are bringing people to your website.

Companies that get the best results from Optimize have a consistent, standardized process for testing in place. This begins when companies generate test ideas. Consider what data sources are available to you from which to draw insights and opportunities for optimization. We recommend looking at your Google Analytics web data for ideas, particularly high-level metrics like transactions, revenue, and abandonment.

If you're an e-commerce site, look at any custom event tracking you've set up, analyzing the data by segments. For example, you might look for audience segments that are lagging behind others. Those are perfect opportunities for optimization. If you have user recordings or heat maps, tools like SessionCam can reveal what users do on your website, providing you with perfect places to start looking for optimization ideas.

Surveys can be used to target users who have abandoned their carts or who search the site for specific products. Ask those users about their experiences to get ideas, then test those ideas. If you're a highly competent organization that is able to generate a ton of ideas, prioritize the tests that are most important for your business objectives. We recommend using a prioritization matrix or a pie chart that identifies the relative impact of potential tests to help you decide which ones to focus on.

Create standard documents for each test that contain information about the changes that are going to be made to your website, the objectives of the test, your hypothesis, and your specific reasons for running the test. Share this document with all departments and make sure everyone is on board before you run the test.

Once the test is complete, create a more in-depth test document to report the results and share it with any department that is either involved or may be impacted by it. Get everyone on the same page so you can move forward with any changes that need to be made.

You should communicate regularly with stakeholders regarding any testing or changes to be implemented. Often, companies think of A/B testing as merely a UX (experience design) function that only needs to be communicated with the marketing team and, depending on the variants being implemented, developers. However, communicating all testing to all stakeholders helps keep your experimentation strategy running smoothly.

You might run into complications if you're working with third-party organizations, especially if their testing methodology isn't ideal. We recommend scheduling a working session with all outside organizations so you can discuss everything each team has already done and what their methodologies have been.

Try to get a sense of who each third-party team member is and what their roles would be during testing. Ask about any marketing or development resources they use, as well as anyone involved in searching their available data sources for ideas. Then you can begin discussing next steps.

WHAT OPTIMIZE LACKS

Understanding what Optimize can do for you is important, but it's just as important to understand the features that it currently lacks.

Big Picture Reporting

If you've experienced growth in your conversion rates in recent weeks due to specific tests you've run, it can be hard to see the big picture without a lot of additional setup. As with most A/B testing tools, you have to log in to Optimize and view results for each experiment individually.

A simple way to see summaries of similar tests or a summary of all tests run within a select time frame would provide a holistic view of the performance of an overall experimentation strategy, but unfortunately, this doesn't exist yet. Although Optimize is part of the Google Marketing Platform, there is currently no connector available for Data Studio, Google's data visualization tool. Consequently, you are only able to display observed conversion rates from Google Analytics as opposed to the modeled conversion rates calculated by Optimize.

Mobile Testing

The Optimize platform doesn't offer the capability of running experiments on mobile apps. However, you can perform A/B testing using Firebase, which is built using the same sophisticated statistics as Optimize. This means that you can still run tests based on Google Analytics data, create variants, and implement changes directly into your app using the Firebase remote configuration cloud service.

Despite lacking a few features, Optimize is a powerful tool to have in your experimentation arsenal, but you must have a solid process in place for continuous testing and improvement across all of your digital platforms. A strong team and communication across departments about this testing will help your organization become far better at identifying and implementing needed changes.

SURVEYS AND SURVEYS 360

Surveys and Surveys 360 are products that recently joined the Google Marketing Platform. Like the other products we've mentioned, it offers both a free version, which is limited to pop-up web satisfaction surveys, and an enterprise version that gives access to showcase surveys both on your website and off-site for more qualitative data collection. Surveys 360 is designed for fast and simple deployment of a qualitative data collection tool on your digital assets and across the web. You can set up a survey in minutes, and results are provided in days rather than the weeks or months of traditional surveys.

The biggest advantage we see with Surveys 360 and why it's so critical to mention with other GMP products is that you can leverage Google Ads remarketing lists to target users who have visited your website or app with surveys as they navigate outside of your digital assets (website or app). For example, when your customers drop off from your website key checkout or registration flow, you can target them to see a specific survey as they navigate to other publisher websites. This can be powerful when building a holistic targeting and audience strategy within GMP between Analytics 360, Campaign Manager, Display & Video 360, and Search Ads 360.

As one of the newer products that integrate with Google Marketing Platform, Surveys is not yet designated as an official part of GMP, though we believe this will change soon. After all, the qualitative data provided by Surveys is a vital part of your marketing toolkit.

SALESFORCE INTEGRATION

I was sitting in the front row at a Google partner summit in Mountain View, California, when Google announced the launch of Universal Analytics. At the time, it was amazing and groundbreaking. As I had spent the first ten years of my career doing systems integrations for some of the biggest companies in the world, my nerdy mind was blown away by the possibilities.

I left Mountain View and, a few months later, attended a meeting in Los Angeles with one of our client companies, a major B2B organization with a large outbound/inbound call center. They were heavy users of Salesforce. Leads came from digital marketing channels, but their sales process was lengthy and rather complex. Consequently, many prospective clients chose to finish the process over the phone.

In the middle of a fun brainstorming session with their executives, a lightbulb went off in my head. What if we used the new Universal Analytics capabilities to build a Salesforce-native module that would send offline engagement and conversions, like over-the-phone orders, to Google Analytics to tie to the online interactions with the website and online marketing efforts that lead to conversion over the phone?

I spent the next couple of days extensively Googling and experimenting to see if anyone had ever done something similar, but I found no evidence of this. Even though I didn't know the Salesforce programming language, Apex, it was close enough to Java that I was able to build a working prototype within a couple of weeks.

The use case was amazing. Prior to this integration, the most you could track in Google Analytics was the cost to generate a lead. However, if you could take a lead, capture it in Salesforce, and then, when the lead converts, send the data back to Google Analytics to track that conversion, you would then be able to track offline sales in GA and truly measure the effectiveness of your media spend. More than that, you could report the purchases of repeat visitors in GA, even if those purchases were made offline. This had never been possible before, and it seemed doable now.

Why is this so important? Because without offline sales, reporting is limited to online sales only, which means KPIs such as *return on ad spend* (ROAS) do not tell the full story. Additionally, you are unable to measure the true value of online marketing and how it impacts all sales, not just online ones.

We partnered with Google on this incredible prototype, and together, we identified an organization where we could pilot this idea. Pelican Water Systems produces cutting-edge, environmentally friendly water filtration and salt-free softening systems. Most of their big-ticket sales were made offline. (As a side note, having been a loyal customer of theirs for the last five years, I must say that their products are fantastic.)

Our pilot produced amazing results:

- The ROI for paid advertising was 130 percent higher than previously measured.
- Fifteen percent of all offline sales were influenced by Google Ads (then called "AdWords").
- Twenty-one percent of all sales started with Google Ads.[13]

Since then, we have implemented this solution for many of our partners, and to this day, I still feel proud that we were the first company in the world to come up with this integration and successfully implement it in production.

ANALYTICS 360 AND SALESFORCE SALES CLOUD

Fast forward a couple of years. As CEO of a company, and I realized one must be proud not just of decisions to say "yes" to things, but also decisions to say "no." I was in love with Salesforce-to-GA integration, but we made a strategic decision not to productize it. So, imagine my excitement when, in 2018, Salesforce announced the general availability of Sales Cloud Data Import with Analytics 360. This automated the solution that we had designed and custom-built for Pelican Water.

13 "Pelican Water System Sees 130% Higher ROI with Google Analytics," Google Analytics Solutions, May 16, 2016, https://services.google.com/fh/files/misc/infotrust-case2.pdf.

Salesforce Sales Cloud Data Import lets you bring sales pipeline data from Sales Cloud directly into Analytics 360. Using Salesforce Sales Cloud Data Import, you can easily augment your digital analytics data with offline sales data (e.g., leads, opportunities, product data, and user attributes). This gives you a more complete picture of the conversion funnel.

You can then measure the value of offline conversions that result from online ad and non-ad clicks without the need to reconcile online and customer relationship management (CRM) data manually. If you have data about customers and their engagement and purchases on a couple of different systems, people might look at the two different datasets and wonder which one to trust to make decisions. Now, however, you can integrate these datasets, unifying them to provide a single view, allowing more streamlined and efficient decisions based on the data you've brought together. With this, you can generate higher ROI.

USE SALESFORCE CLOUD DATA IMPORT TO:

- Track your Salesforce milestones in Analytics 360.
- Gain insights from your data using Analytics 360 segments.
- Grow customer value with remarketing audiences.
- Track performance across all online traffic channels.
- Visualize your user journeys with Custom Funnels.
- Optimize your marketing to Signals such as predicted sales or conversions prior to their occurrence.
- Remarket based on sales data.[14]

---

14 "About Importing Salesforce Sales Cloud Data," Analytics Help, accessed December 28, 2020, https://support.google.com/analytics/answer/7584445.

Analytics 360 + Salesforce Sales Cloud: Details

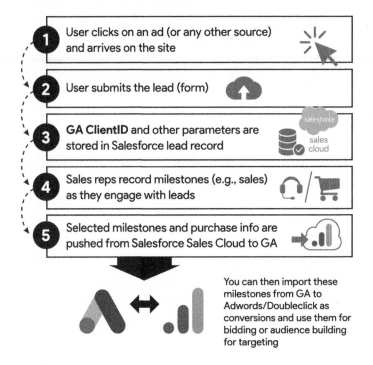

1. User clicks on an ad (or any other source) and arrives on the site

2. User submits the lead (form)

3. **GA ClientID** and other parameters are stored in Salesforce lead record

4. Sales reps record milestones (e.g., sales) as they engage with leads

5. Selected milestones and purchase info are pushed from Salesforce Sales Cloud to GA

You can then import these milestones from GA to Adwords/Doubleclick as conversions and use them for bidding or audience building for targeting

Some important things to keep in mind:

- Sales Cloud Data Import is only available for Analytics 360 users.
- As I've learned from personal experience, Salesforce-to-GA360 integrations can be quite complex. Therefore, product integration only supports standard Salesforce Lead and Opportunity objects, not custom objects. However, there is the ability to include Opportunity Products in the integration as well.

Who is this for?

- B2B big sales items, heavily promoted online but sold

through a dedicated sales team (for example, enterprise software).

- B2C large-ticket consumer items. For example, our friends at Pelican Water Systems with their home water purification system.

Resources:

- Google Analytics knowledge base: support.google.com/ analytics/answer/7584447.

ANALYTICS 360 AND SALESFORCE MARKETING CLOUD

Let's continue exploring the possibilities behind Salesforce and Analytics 360 integration. By combining marketing and analytics information, you can gather meaningful insights and use them in your campaigns. However, it's possible that your customer engagement data is contained in one platform while your performance metrics are contained in another. Fortunately, with Analytics 360 and Salesforce Marketing Cloud, you can easily bring the information from both of these platforms together in order to unify reports, improve the performance of your campaigns, and enjoy more robust analytics.

Integrating Analytics 360 with Salesforce Marketing Cloud enables you to bring the customer website engagement of Analytics 360 into your Marketing Cloud reports, which provides unified reporting for a clearer picture of customer engagement throughout their journey. Previously, if you wanted to measure the performance of an email campaign, you had to use manual tagging, but this integration gives you the ability to add tracking parameters to every email landing page.

This automatically categorizes all outgoing links from your Salesforce Marketing Cloud email campaigns by source, medium, campaign, term, and content required for proper campaign measurement within Analytics 360. Since the integration is two-way, it not only allows metrics to be passed between the systems and campaigns to be properly tracked, it also allows for email and SMS targeting based on data that is not only within the Salesforce Marketing Cloud database about your users but also allows usage of data that may only be within GA360.

THE KEY BENEFITS OF GA360 AND SALESFORCE MARKETING CLOUD INTEGRATION AND AUDIENCE ACTIVATION

By integrating Analytics 360 with Salesforce Marketing Cloud, you can now understand the performance of your email and mobile ad campaigns in light of customer website engagement. Streamline your campaign tagging according to your UTM tagging strategy and unify users across all platforms.

You can also activate your campaigns using GA audiences in Salesforce Marketing Cloud for more enhanced targeting and segmentation. This creates more opportunities to retarget your audiences, consolidate your marketing experiences, and create personalized, multi-moment interactions and experiences using Journey Builder.

With Analytics 360 audiences, you can make your marketing campaigns more relevant to various subgroups within your overall customer base, so when you create ads in Display & Video 360 or Search Ads 360, those selected audiences are immediately available for your Salesforce Marketing Cloud ad campaigns. This enables you to reach channels like email and SMS, creating a seamless experience across all of your brand channels.

Let's take a look at how this might impact your campaigns. If you're running an ad for a product, you can now determine which customers will be most interested in the sale. Maybe they're engaging with the email announcing the product launch, or maybe they've viewed similar products on your website. With Analytics 360, you can create the audience and share it with Salesforce Marketing Cloud. You can also share it in GMP (DV360 or Google Ads) for further customization of your ad.

Also, you can use lookalike audiences in Display & Video 360 based on leads from Salesforce Marketing Cloud, export GA360 data into BigQuery for advanced analysis, and enrich your Marketing Cloud reports with GA360. Ultimately, with all of this, you will drive your organization to digital marketing maturity faster.

The lists of customers maintained in your Salesforce Marketing Campaigns can become your entry source for Journey Builder campaigns, which helps Journey Builder determine where the customers who enter the journey are coming from. Most customer journeys will run on data coming directly from Salesforce. com (SFDC) or a user database with customer attributes. However, Analytics 360 integration allows you to retarget the users exported from the audiences configured in GA360 admin.

These audiences are segments of users captured in GA360 who came to your website from an email or SMS sent through the Journey Builder campaign who have achieved one or more goals on your website. Goals might include filling out contact forms, user registration, adding an item to the cart, or buying a product.

Indeed, the integration of Analytics 360 and Marketing Cloud enables you to create audiences in GA360 using all of the customer engagement data from your apps, websites, and other platforms that you're already collecting to power your campaigns. Bear in mind, it can take up to twenty-four hours for your audiences to show up in Salesforce Marketing Cloud, and you can't use data from Google Signals to create audiences.

ADDITIONAL RESOURCES

https://infotrust.com/crawl-walk-run/

https://infotrust.com/resources/

http://infotrust.com/resource/compliant-tracking-guide-ga4

https://marketingplatform.google.com/about/resources/salesforce-marketing-cloud-integration-feature-brief/

https://support.google.com/analytics/answer/9250031?hl=en

https://help.salesforce.com/articleView?id=mc_gai_google_analytics_integration_tracking.htm&type=5

CHAPTER FIVE

GOOGLE ANALYTICS 4

CHAPTER CONTRIBUTORS: CHRIS VAUGHAN, BRYAN LAMB, AMIN SHAWKI

 Chris Vaughan is the Head of Vertical for CPG, FMCG, and multi-brand partners at InfoTrust, where he helps the world's largest and most recognizable brands develop, deploy, and measure their digital analytics strategies. Through these efforts, Chris has influenced the digital analytics architectures, data collection methodologies, and insights for thousands of websites and mobile apps.

Chris also leads InfoTrust's internal App + Web team, which is currently working to develop strategic guidelines for App + Web properties and to educate our respective client partners on the massive implications of App + Web.

As a husband and father of three girls, Chris enjoys spending time with his family and (whenever possible) working out and reading.

Bryan Lamb is an Analytics Architect at Info-Trust, leading and assisting in the development of analytics architectures and technical solutions for clients. He oversees the company's delivery standards and best practices around the analytics platforms supported by the InfoTrust team, including Google Analytics Universal and recently-released Google Analytics 4. Bryan helps some of the world's most-recognizable brands develop and execute their analytics maturity strategies.

In 2013, Google released the current version of Google Analytics, known throughout the industry as Universal Analytics. When most people talk about Google Analytics today, this is what they're referring to. To prevent confusion, we've used the term "Google Analytics" for most of this book. However, in this section, we will use the term "Universal Analytics" in order to highlight the key differences in features and functionalities between Universal Analytics and the newest iteration: Google Analytics 4 (formerly known as App + Web properties).

THE SHORTCOMINGS OF UNIVERSAL ANALYTICS

Universal Analytics has provided great results for users, but certain limitations have become evident, especially in the last two or three years. When Universal Analytics was rolled out in 2013, people didn't use mobile apps nearly as much as they do today, especially for business purposes. As a result, it wasn't as important for Universal Analytics properties or views to give marketers a 360-degree view of the customer journey across both websites and apps. However, as the impact of mobile devices has risen in our day-to-day lives over the last decade, marketers have begun clamoring for a way to see all of that data brought together in one place.

On top of that, there is an additional pain point. It turns out that mobile apps can collect a *lot* of data since every time a user touches the screen, it can be registered as an event in Universal Analytics. Some organizations with popular apps have had to decide whether to track very granular information about their app usage, potentially exceeding the platform's hit limits, or reduce the amount of data they collect.

Seeing this pain point, Google began offering a different version of analytics tracking for mobile apps through its Firebase mobile development platform. This new product, branded Google Analytics for Firebase, offered unlimited event tracking so organizations can keep up with the massive level of hit data from their apps without having to worry about exceeding hit counts. However, there's a major difference in the foundational data collection model utilized by each of these platforms.

Universal Analytics properties have always utilized a data collection model based around page/screen views and sessions. Of course, data about on-site or in-app user activities can also be tracked with Universal Analytics in the form of "events," but these generally require separate tagging that often must be completed by technical development teams.

On the other hand, Google Analytics for Firebase uses a data collection model that tracks every single activity as an event. This means metrics about activities like viewing a screen or opening the app can be seen alongside data for other event activities, such as tapping a link or scrolling down a page. As a result, marketers don't have to look at screen views or session metrics in one place and event data in another, as with Universal Analytics reports. This is especially important for mobile apps, where so much data is collected.

While that sounds like a great quality of life improvement for assessing the performance of mobile apps, there's still a problem. Not only are marketers unable to easily see how users are utilizing their websites and apps across both types of assets, but the data collected on websites versus apps isn't even using the same data collection model.

This is where the limitation of Universal Analytics has become quite clear, with users running into difficulty when trying to combine different datasets. While dimensions and metrics are unique to each platform, conversion goals are largely the same across devices—a purchase, a sign-up, a download, or any defined objective. With new analytics concepts of user-centricity and micro-moments, digital marketing analysts must now gather and interpret data across devices to fully understand the customer's journey.

Unfortunately, the challenge of data integration has to be overcome before users can begin doing the more exciting advanced analytics that is the hallmark of the "run" phase of marketing. Aware of this, Google began looking for technical changes it could make to the platform to help organizations get to the run stage faster. The end result is called Google Analytics 4.

ENTER GOOGLE ANALYTICS 4

Google Analytics 4 (GA4) is the much-anticipated update of the Google Analytics product, promising to unify tracking and enable data science and artificial intelligence. In this chapter, we will discuss Google Analytics 4 as a platform for cross-device digital marketing and powerful user-centric analytics. There are a number of core differentiators that already exist today and require some additional explanation.

In the first part of this chapter, we will look at the business value of GA4, and then, in the second part, we will look at the technical value proposition and how it works.

THE FUTURE OF ANALYTICS: KEY FINDINGS

According to Forrester Consulting research, cross-platform analytics are still not the norm for a majority of companies using Universal Analytics. Indeed, according to their study, less than half of firms (43 percent) have unified, cross-platform analytics capabilities that can measure customer interactions and map a single solution.[15] GA4's ability to combine data should prove to be a game-changer and will no doubt be one of its biggest selling points.

Another finding of the Forrester Consulting study reveals that decision-makers value privacy features above other analytics platform capabilities, which suggests that decision-makers take a privacy-first view as they seek to protect consumer data and preserve trust. Google Analytics 4 is also bringing a greater focus on privacy and data governance by completely changing the concept of "identity" and how people are tracked across multiple devices. Privacy clearly matters to Google, and it is trying to get ahead of the industry, going beyond privacy regulations to find new, more robust ways to protect people and their data. With GA4, we see it leading the way. To that end,

---

15   "The Future of Analytics," *Forrester Consulting*, July 2020, https://marketingplatform.google.com/about/resources/the-future-of-analytics/.

users can now access data and prevent user events from being used for advertising.

Also, according to the Forrester study, most firms use digital analytics to understand and optimize customer experiences, and improved customer experience is often listed as the top benefit firms have realized from their digital analytics technologies. Eighty-six percent of the decision-makers in the study consider predictive analytics to be critical or very important. Eighty-five percent consider customer journey analytics to be critical or very important, and 84 percent say media activation is critical or very important. In all of these instances, Google Analytics 4 seems poised to help companies better achieve their goals with analytics.

BUSINESS AUDIENCE
DISJOINTED DATASETS

Let's start with a common problem to paint the picture of why GA4 is such an important development. Historically, integrating data has meant identifying commonalities between platforms and creating coherent data sources. However, when companies have attempted to integrate data from different platforms and devices, the process wasted substantial time due to organizing, cleaning, and formatting the data into a machine-readable format to generate rolled-up metrics and dashboards.

Moreover, that process was not as successful in providing actionable insights on how different device interactions collectively led to conversions. *When data gets reduced to commonalities, the richness of the customer's journey is lost.* This was true for classic Google Analytics as well as Universal Analytics. Although websites and apps had similar conversion goals and metrics, sessions didn't match because the concept of a session on a website differed from a session on a mobile app. After all, the way customers utilize apps often differs from the way they browse a website.

Google Analytics 4 solves this by simplifying how user interactions are tracked, using a more flexible approach with events, and introducing the concept of "engaged sessions." Furthermore, GA4 allows analysts to create events from any activity that is relevant to the user experience and attach parameters to record details on that interaction for analysis. This event model creates a common data schema for websites and mobile apps, allowing for quick analysis and visibility into the user journey across devices.

One of the common struggles we've seen in our client organizations is trying to figure out the journeys customers take that lead to conversion. The path is not always clear, but when we ask them, "What steps would you like to see in the analytics reporting," they will often reply, "We want to see them all!"

With Universal Analytics, it's easy to build reports if you know the specific path you want to visualize, but if you're trying to look at every customer path, then it becomes rather clunky. GA4's enhanced user pathing shows various flows that users take, as well as drop off points. It can incorporate various platforms, including apps and websites, to provide a more comprehensive view of what customers are doing (and where they're doing it).

AI-FIRST

The CEO of Google, Sundar Pichai, famously said a few years ago, "I think we will evolve in computing from a mobile-first to an AI-first world. And I do think we are at the forefront of development."

To that end, Google has been thinking about how they can design Google Analytics 4 to help businesses gain faster access to machine learning tools and other cutting-edge technology so they can overcome some of the technical difficulties that have made it harder to get to the "run" phase.

In our experience, many business clients express frustration at how difficult it can be to get simple answers fast from Universal Analytics so they can make better decisions. They don't know where their analytics data is located, or the data is incomplete, or it's scattered across multiple systems. They will sit down to build a dashboard so they can bring all of their data together—something that should be relatively easy—but it turns into a month-long project.

Remember, as an organization, Google's original mission statement was to "organize the world's information." GA4 is intended to help users achieve that mission better by enabling them to collect and organize their data in a way that allows easier and faster access, so marketers can make decisions with more confidence.

To that end, GA4 provides greater capabilities for asking human questions and getting answers directly. Instead of having to ask an analyst for every little detail, the tools themselves now surface the data to users directly. In the old days, asking an analyst for details about your marketing kicked off a whole project in itself, but that is no longer the case.

That doesn't mean there won't still be a need for implementation and restructuring, but it does represent another leap forward.

Indeed, the change from Classic Analytics to Universal Analytics was the first big leap, allowing users to capture data from any device. GA4 is another leap that provides easy and quick access to that data with AI capabilities. Now, you can go to Google Analytics, ask a question about your data, and get an answer almost right away.

This degree of machine learning removes many of the barriers to entry that previously existed when marketers wanted to do amazing things with their data. Formerly, they had to extract their data from Google Analytics, move it to Cloud or BigQuery, write advanced analysis models for it, then move the data back to Google Analytics for activation—a process filled with complexity that required a lot of time and budgetary considerations. It wasn't something a company could accomplish in the "crawl" stage of analytics maturity.

Of course, these are just the tip of the iceberg in terms of what's going to be available once machine learning and AI have fully developed the ability to make predictions based on data. Marketers will be able to use these predictions to run tests without the need for data scientists or cloud experts and without the elaborate schemes they had to use before.

That's not to say that data scientists will no longer be needed. On the contrary, the AI capabilities of GA4 will drive more demand for them because once users have the ability to test things for themselves and see the results, advanced analytics of those results will become even more important. Still, the fact that marketers can test the validity of predictions themselves right in GA4 is an exciting development.

With Universal Analytics, if you were looking for an answer, you could go into an event report, but you had to know in advance what the data in the report meant. Data was contained in three fields: category, action, and label. GA4, on the other hand, is more focused on what people are doing, which means when you look at an event, more context is provided for the data.

You can analyze an event report without the need to create some kind of architectural guide. Labels tell you exactly what the data represents, so you can immediately identify an event by its name. The data parameters that are collected are also defined by what they represent, so you can look at a report and instantly understand what the data means. This makes the analysis of data vastly easier.

There's a lot more customization as well, so organizations can track data in a way that is far more specific to their needs. Indeed, it allows *both* standardization of data and white-space customization at the same time. While the data collection process is very flexible, you can create a highly structured system in the UI if you wish.

With Universal Analytics, the platform was essentially "off the shelf." You just added tracking to your website and received reports. Now, however, there is a whole suite of reports available under the Analysis Hub that is customizable. You can build almost any kind of report you want, creating events of any activity relevant to the user experience and attaching parameters to record details of that interaction. This event model creates a common data schema for websites and mobile apps, allowing for a compliant, AI-first analysis and visibility into the user journey across devices.

In a sense, GA4 is both simpler *and* more complex, depending on what you prefer, making it well-suited for the crawl, walk, and run stages of analytics maturity. You get all of the "out-of-the-box" tracking that Google is known for, even enhanced events, combined with "blank slate" customizations to meet your organization's needs.

In our opinion, fast adoption of GA4 to drive data collection and model maturity will allow Google to speed up the training of its machine learning models, which will improve the quality of predictions and accelerate the path to AI-based media buying. Thus, it's only going to get better over time.

NEW REPORTING CAPABILITIES

Since the new reporting capabilities of Google Analytics 4 are poised to be such a significant change for users, let's dive a little deeper into some of the improvements. As we mentioned, GA4 is less about creating standard reports and more about analyzing data to find answers to specific questions. With Universal Analytics, you could layer some custom data over the top of your standard report, but with GA4, you're more focused on analysis and exploration of the data.

By tracking users across devices, reports can paint a clearer picture of their behavior along the customer journey. Instead of a focus on page views or sessions, the focus is now on user-based insights based on events and interactions. As a result, you can also get a clearer idea of what users are doing, which is called "intent-based analysis." You see not just what users are clicking or viewing, but what they're trying to do.

Since GA4's new event-based architecture will encourage a mindset shift in users, from "What are people seeing?" to

"What are people doing?" this potentially introduces a whole new direction for analytics. After all, page views don't tell you much about what people are actually doing. With Universal Analytics, you know if they're looking at a page, but that doesn't tell you if they are actually consuming the information on the page or engaging in some way.

Ultimately, page views are little more than a vanity metric. With GA4, users have the ability to focus on what people are actually doing and how they are engaging with the content on the page. Even basic interactions, like a user scrolling down the screen, can be tracked easily.

Consider this scenario: Two customers of a retail website started their journey on the same channel—clicking a promotion on Facebook—but then took different paths to conversion between different channels and devices. One ended up converting on the retailer's website, while the other made the purchase on the retailer's mobile app. With an event-based model, the interactions from different devices are automatically merged together.

Another advantage of GA4, due to its simplified model, is that the volume of data that is collected will be less of a problem for users. For consumption-based businesses, in particular, this should be helpful since the large volume of data they typically want to collect will be more feasible. For example, let's suppose a company wanted to track view-length on videos, creating a report that shows viewership in ten-second intervals. In Universal Analytics, the sheer volume of data would become a bottleneck, but GA4 can handle the volume with no problem.

Also, for the first time, GA4 makes *funnels* available for everyone. Previously, Google Analytics had very rigid funnels in the standard version, with only GA360 providing customizable funnels. You can build custom funnels on the fly that are retroactive, segmentable, and allow you to create audiences for deeper exploration or activation.

Google Analytics 4 still offers the power of retargeting campaigns through integrations with other platforms. This has been a promise of Google since they first got into analytics, but the more robust data connection analysis reporting should integrate even more powerfully with advertising technology. As of the writing of this book, this is still a work in progress, but we feel confident in saying that Google will maintain most of its current integrations with other marketing platform products and tools, and they might become even more flexible and efficient.

Thus, users shouldn't lose any of the capabilities they have currently with Universal Analytics, and they may very well find that they were even better, especially if integrations are easier to deploy. At this stage, some of this is speculation, but it seems likely that GA4 will lower the barrier of entry for integrations.

Even with Universal Analytics, the ease with which it is integrated with other products in Google's Marketing Platform, such as Search 360 or Display & Video 360, was already a selling point. If GA4 manages to lower the barrier of entry even further, it should become an even more attractive option.

TECHNICAL AUDIENCE: DEEPER DIVE

As we explained earlier, Google Analytics 4 uses an event-based model for tracking all user interactions, and while the concept of event data modeling is not new to analytics platforms, Google has its own specifics and customizations for the event model. With previous versions of Google Analytics, events had a rigid, though minor, role in the tracking model. Everything revolved around *sessions* and *hits*, making the switch to events a major breakthrough. While this measurement model is new for websites, it's not new for mobile apps, as GA4 utilizes the same data schema as Google Analytics for Firebase, Google's standard for tracking mobile app analytics for the past three years.

In general, event data modeling tracks user actions then adds meaning to the collected information through analysis. For example, an "add to cart" event might be an indication of a customer's interest in a certain product category when evaluating interests and segmenting users. On the other hand, the same "add to cart" event could be the first step in a purchase funnel when analyzing checkout behavior.

Event data models collect data points for each user action through event parameters. The analysis of customer behavior then involves applying business logic to uncover insights at the user level. Event data models have two levels of hierarchy for data collection: *User* and *Event* (including parameters that are unique to each event). They collect information specific to the user profile, which forms the user properties, including identifiers across platforms such as a user ID or membership type.

Session data contains information about the platform the user is on during their session, such as the *browser, device,* and *referral source,* as well as event data or parameters based on the action tracked. For example, e-commerce events may include product information, whereas engagement events will include information on clicked items and their placement. GA4 uses the concept of custom dimensions for event parameters to include details on the tracked event.

Example of Event Structure in an Event Stream

Event Name	User ID	Platform	Event Parameters	(Custom Dimensions)	Timestamp	
app_download	1111567	app	OS, version, source	2020-10-16	23:10:04
model_click	2222564	web	browser, device, cta	2020-10-17	23:10:04
add_to_cart	1111567	web	product details	2020-10-17	23:12:04
purchase	2222564	web	transaction info, products	2020-10-17	23:10:04
add_to_cart	1111567	app	product details	2020-10-19	23:10:04
purchase	1111564	app	transaction info, products	2020-10-20	23:10:04

More robust forecasting will be possible in GA4 thanks to a couple of things.

First, the new user ID architecture will make it easier to track people across platforms because you're looking at *people* now, not *page views*. Using user IDs with Google Signals to aggregate data inside of GA4, without the need for an external system, will enable new types of analysis based on real human behavior.

Second, being able to track user lifetime value across platforms will empower predictive models in a way not seen before. Whether they were on desktop, mobile, iPad, or smartphone, you will see separate pieces of data tied together to provide a look at an individual user's lifetime experience with your organization.

GA4's *user graph* gives a clear picture of that lifetime value, powering predictions even further. In your analysis, it provides a holistic view of what users are doing on various devices. It also makes use of audiences more efficiently, which should be a welcome improvement for marketers who have typically struggled in the past to build audiences that excluded people who'd already converted. Being able to tie activity to specific users and devices should help tremendously with this.

Recently, we provided a client with a list of their customers who had a high lifetime value so they could target them. This proved to be highly valuable to them, and they had great success. However, a couple months later, they asked us: "How many of the people on this list would have converted anyway? In other words, are they truly our highest lifetime value customers, or were they already going to buy and just happened to wind up on this list?"

It was an interesting question and one that could not be easily answered with Universal Analytics. However, GA4's ability to track user behavior from device to device might provide the clarity our client sought by providing a holistic picture of that customer's behavior.

In the past, companies typically exported the data from Google, conducted their own customer lifetime value analysis externally, then brought that data back into Universal Analytics. While this worked fine for many people, these kinds of integrations always have some inefficiencies in terms of people, processes, and platforms. Any time you move data from one platform to another or have to rely on a lot of manual analysis, you need to introduce more resources to get it done the right way.

Now, the ability to produce accurate customer lifetime value datasets within Google Analytics 4 means you should be able to eliminate those inefficiencies and make the data actionable practically in real time. The cost, in terms of time, people, and resources, should be dramatically lower because all of the information you need is now readily available within GA4.

At a time when COVID is still impacting so many business communities, we still don't know what the next "normal" is going to look like, so getting as much ROI from your campaigns as possible, as soon as possible, is critical. We need the ability to experiment faster, and having access to the predictive data that GA4 offers can help us expedite some things.

With more advanced capabilities inside GA4, data scientists and engineers can spend less time building simple models and more time doing advanced work in developing the next generation of models and more difficult, complex analysis, removing constraints that keep organizations from moving forward.

ENHANCED MEASUREMENT FOR WEBSITES

When you create a data stream for a website in your GA4 property, GA4 gives you the ability to activate a new feature called "Enhanced Measurement." This awesome new functionality allows organizations to automatically track key interactions on their websites out of the box without any additional code implementations.

Available interactions that are able to be tracked include some of the most common website activities, including:

- Page Views
- Scrolls

- Outbound Link Clicks
- Site Searches
- File Downloads
- Video Engagement (YouTube only)

Previously, implementing tracking for some of these activities would have required setting up separate tags or deploying on-site code changes through a development team. However, with the new "Enhanced Measurement" feature, this data can all be available to you with just the toggle of a setting in your website Data Stream.

ABILITY TO MODIFY EXISTING EVENTS

You can also modify existing events that you have implemented without the need to go back and update your web or app tagging. This can be used to fix casing issues and/or spelling mistakes. Plus, you can use this feature to create new events from an existing event, which enables you to set up custom conversions by creating new events from something you care about, like an outbound link click.

DATA STREAMS IN GA4: ENABLING DATA SCIENCE

In 2018, *Harvard Business Review* published a report about using analytics to improve customer engagement.[16] The key takeaway from the report is that "more sources provide more value." The report goes on to discuss how analytics innovators take advantage of multiple data sources to glean new customer insights and deepen their relationship with customers.

---

16   Sam Ransbotham and David Kiron, "Using Analytics to Improve Customer Engagement," *MIT Sloan Management Review* (April 2018), https://store.hbr.org/product/using-analytics-to-improve-customer-engagement/SMR671.

GA4 introduces the concept of data "streams" to indicate the different pipelines of data coming from different platforms. Streams can be websites or mobile applications, and multiple websites or mobile apps can be defined as streams coming into the same GA4 property, providing the ability for cross-device and cross-platform measurement.

Reporting within the GA4 interface allows for analysis across all streams or within a specific data stream if you're looking to analyze a specific platform. This is a significant point of difference from the previous approach, in which a lot of mapping had to be done before analysts were able to "roll-up" multiple websites or apps together.

Businesses that can easily connect users across devices and websites instantly reap the benefits of unified tracking by using data-driven attribution. They are also able to quickly act on the data. Having user-level data on all user actions in one place allows analysts to understand how customers navigate across touchpoints as they move through the user journey. Companies can then better anticipate the customer's needs, expectations, and desires during each part of the journey.

BIGQUERY EXPORT

Google Analytics 4 provides the ability to integrate and stream data into BigQuery. Prior to GA4, with Universal Analytics, this integration was only available for Analytics 360 Enterprise Edition, but the BigQuery integration now allows you to move your raw event data directly into a Cloud Platform-based data warehouse. Refer to our chapter on Google Cloud for more information.

The new streaming export of GA4 is significantly faster than the current export for GA360, which is only updated every ten to fifteen minutes. Plus, you now have the option to choose where you want to store your data to comply with your data governance frameworks.

USER PROPERTIES AND USER ID FOR CROSS-PLATFORM ANALYSIS

You may already be familiar with the term "user-scoped dimension" from Universal Analytics properties. These dimensions allow you to track attributes about the individuals who visit your website without the need to set those attributes on every page. In GA4 properties, these user-scoped dimensions are now called "user properties."

User properties are attributes that describe the individuals using your website or app that rarely change. For instance, the geographic area where a user lives (e.g., continent, country, metro area) or the language they've set in their browser.

Sites with user login, registration, or purchase functionalities may choose to collect additional user properties, such as the unique ID of the user who logs in to the website or app. They may also want to track unique attributes like the loyalty type of the user in order to segment reporting and see if there are differences in how "Gold" loyalty users utilize the website or app versus how "Silver" users utilize it.

This kind of cross-platform analysis sounds amazing, but what makes it possible to stitch together user sessions across different devices? As it turns out, the reporting identity in GA4 properties is completely different from those in Universal Analytics.

While Universal Analytics forces you to choose between analyzing your users based on their anonymous IDs in one place or using your own User IDs, GA4 takes a completely new approach and also provides a huge upgrade. By default, it now uses all identities at once, taking a waterfall approach. First, it uses your own User IDs. Then, if those aren't available, it uses Google Signals (Google's Identity Graph).

The addition of Signals, which can now power all of your reports, will be particularly beneficial to users who don't have their own User Ids for logged-in users. You can also change between the reporting identities since the setting is ad hoc, retroactive, and doesn't make any permanent changes to your data.

If neither of those are available, it falls back on anonymous device IDs. This method uses either analytics cookies for websites or the app-instance ID for apps to identify a user and ignores any user IDs that were collected.

USER LIFETIME

The real power in all of this is the ability to see the big picture, leveraging user ID and Google Signals to look at all user data across all devices in order to "see" all purchases and other conversions and engagements across as one dataset. You no longer have to export out of GA into BigQuery in order to aggregate all lifetime behavior and make forecasting decisions based on the data.

With a full lifetime view aggregated across all devices, you can now:

- Find channels or campaigns that bring the highest lifetime revenue users.

- Understand who your active users are, their journey over the last thirty days, and when they were last measured.
- Identify the first interaction, engagement, or purchase made by a user.
- Identify the most recent interactions and the data associated with the last time a user was measured for a property. For example, their last activity or purchase date.
- Find channels or campaigns that bring the highest purchase probability or the lowest churn probability users.

Note: Lifetime data is available for users who have been active on your site or app after August 15, 2020. For these users, the scope of the data in the user lifetime includes all of their data since they first visited your site or app. Find more information here: https://support.google.com/analytics/answer/9947257

PREDICTIVE CAPABILITIES AND MACHINE LEARNING MODELS

By applying Google's advanced machine learning models, the new analytics capabilities can automatically alert you to significant trends in your data, such as products with rising demand because of new customer needs.

In the past, as we said, we relied on BigQuery to aggregate user data, deliver advanced forecasts and models, and put the results back into GA for data activation. With GA4's improved ability to look at all user data across all devices, we now have a much richer dataset to run built-in machine learning models against to anticipate future actions your customers may take.

For example, new metrics can calculate churn probability so you can more efficiently invest in retaining customers at a time when marketing budgets are under pressure. This allows you to create audiences to reach higher-value customers and run analyses to better understand why some customers are likely to spend more than others, so you can take action to improve your results.

Note: For more information, check out the following article: https://blog.google/products/marketingplatform/analytics/new-predictive-capabilities-google-analytics/

Google Analytics 4 automatically enriches your data by bringing machine learning expertise to bear on your dataset to predict the future behavior of your users. With predictive metrics, you learn more about your customers just by collecting structured event data. The predictive metrics we're talking about include the following:

- **Purchase Probability**: predicts the likelihood that users who have visited your website or app in the last twenty-eight days will purchase in the next seven days.
- **Churn Probability**: predicts how likely it is that recently active users will *not* visit your website or app in the next seven days.
- **Revenue Prediction**: the revenue expected from all purchase conversions within the next twenty-eight days from a user who was active in the last twenty-eight days.

GA4 also includes new predictive audiences that you can create in the Audience Builder.

Here are some of the capabilities we predict will soon be available for Enterprise Analytics (Analytics 360) from *inside* GA4. These are not available at the time of publishing, but we believe they will be in the near future:

- Create an audience of high-value, high-purchase probability or high-revenue prediction customers in Analytics 360 and reach it in your D&V Campaigns.
- Gain valuable insights directly from customers by creating an audience in Analytics 360 made up of customers who have low-revenue prediction or high-churn probability and find out why with Surveys 360.
- Identify audiences with high-churn probability to activate in Salesforce Marketing Cloud to send a special deal.

HOW GOOGLE ANALYTICS 4 HELPS MARKETERS

Marketers want to know their customers in order to build relationships with them, but demographics and psychographics won't help predict a customer's next action. Behavioral data about users is significantly better for predicting things like purchases, upgrades, and churn.

What the customers do paints a better picture of their next action than who they are. Therefore, the key to understanding customers is knowing their actions across channels and showing them what they expect or need at each moment—the ability to answer before they ask!

By using events to track user interactions seamlessly across platforms in GA4, analysts can merge device data together to create a robust picture of the customer's journey and visualize marketing effectiveness. Also, as event-based models simplify data collection in GA4, marketers can now perform analysis at a massive scale and in a timely manner.

Through predictive analytics and machine learning tools, unified customer data from all channels provides the next actionable insight. An example is data from over-the-top (OTT) applications, such as Netflix or Hulu. Previously, getting analytics from these devices to merge into the customer profile of the website or app usually took many hours, with some data lost in transition. By the time insights became available, it was too late to execute on some campaigns.

Conversely, when all platforms have a common "skip-video" event that they track, the data is simpler to query, and user behavior becomes available in real time. This facilitates instant insights for action. A customer who skipped portions of a sitcom on their TV (with OTT) might quickly now be provided with a new viewing suggestion when they open the app on their phone.

In regard to OTT, bear in mind that GA4 doesn't really have a software development kit (SDK) for these platforms yet, though it will probably be possible to send data using GMP. We've just begun having some early conversations about this with our clients.

GA4 easily incorporates new products and experiences. Having unified events across platforms with different parameters provides the capability of storing data in an unstructured or semi-structured manner, making a flexible and scalable model that can take in new parameters and new events.

For example, the "add to cart" event referred to in the table earlier in this chapter has a different set of parameters when tracked in-app versus on the website. Depending on how and where the addition to the cart happens, it can track different data points. This is important for businesses that offer new features or use different tools because they frequently find themselves needing to incorporate new events or measure new custom dimensions only on specific platforms.

The stitching of user interaction across devices demands a common identifier, such as the user. For anonymous users, Google still provides other methods to stitch sessions and provide insights. As users sign in to their Google accounts on different devices, GA4 can recognize the cross-device user journeys and also remarket to the same user in cross-device eligible remarketing campaigns. This can be achieved by enabling the Google Signals feature in GA4.

MIGRATING TO GOOGLE ANALYTICS 4

So, what does migration to Google Analytics 4 look like? At this point, you're probably wondering how painful it's going to be. What will you need in terms of people, and what will the processes look like if you decide to make the switch?

When you present the idea of migration to your team, no doubt you will receive a range of questions about it, so we want to provide you with answers. We will also create a short, bulleted list for easy access. For now, let's examine the process of migration to GA4 in terms of people, processes, and platforms.

Phases of GA4 Deployment

Phase + Estimated Duration	Description of Migration Step
PHASE 1 Estimated Duration: 2–4 weeks	Development of holistic GA4 tracking strategy across Enterprise's digital assets, in conjunction with organizational stakeholders • Recommended "dual-tracking" strategy (in conjunction with existing UA tracking) for events and activities on websites: Visit our website at *https://infotrust.com/crawl-walk-run* to download a template of the Data Migration Plan for Universal Analytics to Google Analytics 4 • Recommended tracking strategy for events and activities on mobile apps
PHASE 2 Estimated Duration: Varies based on development team	• Deployment and configuration of Google Analytics assets necessary to match approved GA4 tracking strategy • Setup/configuration of Firebase or App+Web project to match approved strategic analytics elements (events, custom parameters, user properties) (if applicable)
PHASE 3 Estimated Duration: 2–4 weeks	• Comprehensive testing and debugging to ensure reliable collection of GA4 data across owned website and mobile app

For your team, it won't be much different than a regular implementation. You will need members of your tech/dev to assist because you will need to make changes to your website and tag management system in order to add GA4. Then you will need your analytics and marketing teams. GA4 uses a different data model, so they will need to create some processes to move from the way you were collecting data before to the way it is collected in GA4. This may entail a holistic conversation about how different departments are currently using the data. We recommend keeping it simple and talking about event collection: how individual departments perceive it, how they've been using it, and so on.

Since they will be migrating from an event model of "category, action, label" to an event model with one or more parameters, your internal discussion will need to address what that's going to look like. Once you've mapped a process for how you're going to use that data in GA4, you can begin working with your technical teams on how you're going to do the full migration and what it's going to take.

Depending on how robust your deployment of Universal Analytics is, your tag management systems and data layers and how you collect data may already be decoupled from how you make it available across your organization. In that case, your migration from Universal Analytics to GA4 may require relatively less effort. After all, you're relying on the same data; you're simply packaging it differently for GA4.

On the other hand, if you don't have a tag management system, your migration might be significantly more difficult because of your greater dependency on developers to make changes happen. They will need to create some code for your website, after all.

We recommend taking a *crawl, walk, run* phased approach to your GA4 migration. To start, just get the base tag on your website, so you can start collecting the various kinds of data that GA4 is suited for right out of the box. Maybe include some enhanced reporting. Even if it isn't initially finely tuned for your business, just start collecting relevant data about your website into a GA4 property. That way, your analysts and marketing team can start getting comfortable with the different approach. They will need to learn how analysis and reporting work in GA4.

Establishing a base comfort level will help them make the

mental shift from Universal Analytics to Google Analytics 4, dipping their toes in the water, so when you're ready to take the next step and bring all of your data into GA4, you will already have taught them the new platform. Depending on how friendly your current infrastructure is with GA4, you may need time for some long-term planning to get yourself to a point where GA4 is your sole "source of truth," collecting only what you're doing from a business perspective.

When making your migration, don't forget about the six Ps. Above all, don't lose sight of your *purpose* for moving to GA4. This is the perfect opportunity to step back and reevaluate the role of analytics in your organization. Some of our clients have spent years investing in their current analytics platform, so they've reached the connected or multi-moment stage. Now, they have a whole new platform to learn about.

Gaining clarity about this will create an alignment that will make migration easier within your organizations. We recently spoke to a large enterprise with hundreds of websites and properties. They've spent years building the infrastructure for their many brands and websites, but they've gotten to a point where they feel good about it. Consequently, they are reluctant about moving to GA4. They are a slow-moving enterprise, and like a huge ship, turning in a new direction would normally take a very long time.

However, migration to GA4 provides the perfect opportunity for them to reevaluate the purpose of their analytics organization. In terms of the complexity for an enterprise of that size, they can take it one step at a time, starting migration with dual-tagging on a single brand website. They might even choose one of their savvier brands since they're more likely to buy in to the value of GA4 and take the next leap in analytics maturity. That first brand website can become the internal flagship for migration.

In other words, if you're a large, complex organization with many websites, start small and scale it out. That's another form of "crawl, walk, run." The longer you overlap data collection between two analytics platforms, the more you will come to understand baseline measurements. Over time, you will gain more confidence in data collection, ensuring that the new platform data matches the old. You will also have time to make the mindset shift to Google Analytics 4.

ADDITIONAL RESOURCES

Google's upgrade to GA4 guide: https://support.google.com/analytics/answer/9744165?hl=en&ref_topic=9303319.

Universal Analytics new user guide: https://support.google.com/analytics/answer/10089681?hl=en&ref_topic=9143232.

Be sure to check our website regularly for more information about GA4 developments. New features and functionalities are being released each month, and we'll be sure to keep you informed of any breaking news at infotrust.com/crawl-walk-run.

CHAPTER SIX

ATTRIBUTION/ MEDIA MIX MODELING

CHAPTER CONTRIBUTOR: AMIN SHAWKI

"Half the money I spend on advertising is wasted; the trouble is I don't know which half."

—JOHN WANAMAKER

Conversion attribution is the practice advertisers use to give appropriate credit to every impression, interaction, or click that helps drive a conversion in a campaign. It provides a way of giving credit to the different marketing activities, both online or offline, that motivate customers to recognize your brand and do something you want them to do on your digital platforms.

Today's shoppers see countless signals and messages from the advertisers and brands they're interested in, both online (through search, social media, and email marketing) and offline (through television, billboards, in-store placements, word of mouth, and more). In this chapter, we will look at how attribution works for companies today, how it is used in relation to digital measurements, and what the future holds.

For many organizations, attribution has proved to be quite a challenge. When done right, it can unite people and processes to achieve a faster pace with your digital marketing decisions, speeding you toward payoff by allowing you to invest in the most profitable and valuable marketing channels. However, without the right people and processes in place to enable the technology, it can be difficult and even dangerous, producing incorrect outputs that lead to wasted investments.

Companies typically begin exploring attribution during the *walk* phase of their digital analytics journey, while they are in the *connected* maturity stage. Doing attribution analysis and making decisions based on this data correctly and regularly has the potential of moving your organization from *walk* to *run*, from *connected* to *multi-moment*.

Let's look at the components of attribution and examine how you can get started.

WHO DESERVES THE CREDIT?

By the time a consumer decides to make a purchase or perform an action such as filling out an online form, they have probably already been exposed to dozens, if not hundreds, of different signals and touchpoints with your brand. Attribution tries to showcase the value of all of the interactions that led to that conversion or key action.

Suppose an advertiser sells a product on their own website. Here's a possible scenario for how a customer converts:

- While getting ready to meet a friend, he sees a TV ad showcasing the brand's key product.
- He decides to conduct a Google search on the product, clicking on an ad that leads to the brand's website. However, he is late meeting his friend, so he closes the browser before doing anything else.
- Later that day, on the way home from meeting with his friend, he sees a billboard for the same company.
- After arriving at home, he logs on to Facebook and sees an ad for the same product. This reminds him to look at the brand website, so he clicks the Facebook ad. After navigating the website a bit, he finally decides to buy the product.

As you can see, the customer saw three or four different signals from the company before making a purchase. Which one gets credit for the conversion? Should it be the initial TV ad that introduced the customer to the brand and inspired further research? Should it be the Google ad that reinforced that interest? Then again, it was the Facebook ad that ultimately led to the purchase. Maybe the brand website deserves the most credit since that is where the customer ultimately committed to buying the product. What is the value of each of the touchpoints that led to conversion?

Attribution helps you answer those questions, giving value to each touchpoint on the road to conversion, so you know where to spend your time, energy, and investments to drive more people to convert.

THE BASIC FORMULA OF ATTRIBUTION

What makes attribution so difficult is the vast number of ways that customers get exposed to your brand, product, or service prior to making a purchase. Fortunately, in regard to digital channels, it has become a bit easier in the last few years, thanks to the digital measurement technology provided by Google Analytics, Adobe Analytics, and other measurement-focused platforms.

For digital attribution to work, you need two basic inputs.

First, you need *conversions*, which refers to the ultimate action you want customers to make. Which customer actions showcase success? Is it purchasing a product, signing up for a service, or something else?

Second, you need the digital touchpoints that bring customers to the point of conversion, including acquisition channels such as email, social media, organic and paid search, affiliates, and any other online resource that moves customers to conversion. In other words, where are customers coming from?

With these two basic ingredients, any organization can conduct simple attribution. Google Analytics (and most measurement platforms today, for that matter) automatically shows you a form of attribution in its basic report. These are called *last touch attribution*, and they are available on the platform right out of the box. However, they only show you the last interaction a customer had before conversion, and 100 percent of the credit is given to that last touchpoint. In our previous example, Google Analytics would have given Facebook 100 percent of the credit for that sale.

Another common model is *first touch attribution*, which, in our example, would give all of the credit to the Google paid search ad that first brought the customer to the brand's website, even if the purchase didn't happen at that time. The advantage of first touch attribution is that it can reveal all of the different channels, campaigns, and investments that play a role in the customer journey. Between these two models, *last touch attribution* is the default, but *first touch attribution* can be toggled on and off.

These two models can make you look at your digital channels very differently. For example, if you only look at last touch, you might see that Google organic is strong at driving conversions, while paid search and display ads are not as impactful. However, when you look at first touch, you realize that paid search and display ads are often a customer's initial interaction with your brand.

If you look only at last touch, you might decide, "Let's not invest in paid search or display ads because they don't drive conversion." In reality, you are hurting your engagement with customers.

Another attribution model available through Google Analytics is *linear attribution*, which gives equal credit to every touchpoint on the customer journey. In our example, if the final purchase was $100, then linear attribution would credit $25 to each of the four touchpoints along the customer journey.

You can also use a *time-decay-based attribution* model, which gives more credit to the channels that bring users to your website since this gets them closer to conversion. Beyond these models, you can create your own custom attribution, so if you are a sophisticated organization, you can map out the value of touchpoints in the customer journey however you see fit.

DATA-DRIVEN ATTRIBUTION

Fortunately, the enterprise edition of Google Analytics has advanced capabilities to help you determine which attribution model makes the most sense for your marketing analysis. Google will provide you with machine learning models that automatically determine what value should be assigned to individual channels or campaigns based on the user conversion data. They will even leverage all of the costs across your channels, as long as you have available ad spend data, to calculate the investment value of each touchpoint on the journey to conversion.

With this data, the machine learning algorithm will assign a recommended value to each channel, bringing users to your website. This is called the *data-driven attribution* model, and we recommend clients use it alongside *first touch* and *last touch* to get the most complete picture of where to invest your marketing efforts.

Beyond looking at attribution models, it can be helpful to create a visual of some kind that shows all of your channels and campaigns and how they are converting. Visual reports reveal the sequence of touchpoints leading to conversion in a way that is easy to wrap your head around, which can be helpful when deciding where to invest.

CHANNEL-SPECIFIC ATTRIBUTION

We do not recommend relying on channel-specific attribution tools. Facebook and Twitter, for example, have their own default attribution tools, but they only provide conversion data on their individual channels.

Suppose User A clicks on a Facebook ad, then clicks an organic search, before finally converting on your website, while User B only looks at organic search before converting from Google. If you use Facebook's default attribution tool, it would only report User A's path to conversion and not give credit to the organic search click in the sequence at all. There is no cross-channel attribution reporting. You could, of course, look at multiple single-channel attribution tools, but that creates needless complications.

Through Google Analytics, you can see cross-channel engagement for all channels and sources of traffic that are bringing users to your site for a more complete picture of conversion attribution.

MEDIA MIX MARKETING

Digital measurement is fairly easy as long as you have the right acquisition tracking in place. Where it gets tricky is when you apply impression data with a click to your website. Interactions with your brand through TV commercials, billboards, and other nondigital impressions like in-store interactions with customer service are difficult to incorporate into your digital attribution models.

If you want to incorporate an offline channel, *media mix marketing* provides a better process. Media mix marketing focuses holistically on the impact of all touchpoints, online and offline, that drive conversion, though it lacks the amount of detail that you get from digital attribution.

There are other methods for bringing your ad data across all touchpoints, online and offline, into a single database. For example, you can use Cloud for Marketing to run customer lifetime value (CLV) modeling to predict customer engagement and assign a high-value, medium-value, and low-value score to each channel. From there, you can decide where to invest. It's a different way to look at attribution, but it can be effective. See our chapter on Cloud for Marketing for more information on CLV modeling.

AN UNCERTAIN FUTURE FOR ATTRIBUTION

In the future, attribution will almost certainly become more challenging. Digital attribution relies largely on both first-party and third-party cookies, which store information about user interactions. When a user visits your website, a cookie assigns them an ID, so when they return to the website later from a different traffic source, your measurement platform recognizes them as the same user. Those sessions are tied together to create a clear picture of the customer journey.

While first-party cookies are written and stored directly on your website, third-party cookies follow users around the internet. You can read more about tags and cookies in our customer data governance chapter. The key here is that privacy regulations like GDPR and CCPA, as well as browser-specific privacy changes like Apple's Intelligent Tracking Prevention (ITP), Mozilla's Enhanced Tracking Protection (ETP), and most recently, Google Chrome's elimination of third-party cookies altogether by 2022, are making it more difficult—if not impossible—to rely on cookies for attribution (of impressions primarily) by restricting how cookies are written and stored, what information they can include, and how long they can persist before automatically being deleted.

While the goal is to protect customer privacy, the consequence is that marketers will find it harder to analyze user interactions across the web that drive conversions online. Modern browsers have essentially eliminated the ability to use third-party cookies, and even first-party cookies have severe limits to their life span—sometimes, as short as one day—before they are auto-deleted.

If a user comes to your website from a Facebook ad, browses for a while, and then returns to your website two weeks later from a Google search and converts, there's no real way to tie those two sessions together. The organic search will get all of the credit for the conversion.

Dealing with these restrictions requires thinking about attribution differently. Different forms of analysis need to be explored, using data to make educated guesses about which channels were involved in a customer's journey to conversion. Ultimately, as with any marketing, the best course of action in this changing landscape is to run tests. In whatever process you are using to measure your marketing investments, combine the available data with media mix marketing and run tests to see if it drives your bottom line.

You can reallocate some of your budget from one campaign to another, assessing the performance of individual campaigns using different attribution models. Make changes along the way and observe the impact on your conversion rate.

Above all, don't get discouraged. Marketing technology will continue to evolve. As long as you have a clear purpose for your digital analytics, along with the right people and processes to achieve that purpose, you will still be able to fulfill the needs of your business and achieve success.

To learn more about App + Web, check out our resources at infotrust.com/crawl-walk-run.

CHAPTER SEVEN

GOOGLE CLOUD FOR MARKETING

CHAPTER CONTRIBUTORS: PAM CASTRICONE, TYLER BLATT, ARIEL OPELT

Pam Castricone is Head of Data Science at Info-Trust, where she helps e-commerce retailers and CPG organizations uncover greater insights and value from their data assets. Specializing in statistical and machine learning models, she applies these advanced analytical techniques to drive better ROI than traditional methods. As a Google Cloud Certified Professional Data Engineer, Pam also helps her clients put their models into production in the cloud to drive long-term usability and success.

Pam is an adjunct instructor at the University of Cincinnati's Lindner College of Business, where she teaches a graduate-level course on digital analytics with her colleague, Andy Gibson, who is also a contributor to this book. When she isn't analyzing data, Pam enjoys reading, the arts, and going out for brunch.

In his five years at InfoTrust, Tyler Blatt has brought the concept of full-stack developer to the analytics and marketing world. Starting with tag implementation and finishing with data warehouse creation, he has covered the full scope of the analytics data life cycle. He is currently Head of Integrations at InfoTrust, where he works with his team to tackle the problems of siloed data, data science, and ETL services.

We invited Pam, Tyler, and Ariel to coauthor this chapter in order to share some of their wisdom and experience from building real-time forecasting engines for the largest global consumer packaged goods companies, which has been compared to "upgrading an engine on a moving bus of enterprise marketing architecture while going sixty miles per hour without missing a beat."

In this chapter, we will look at a platform that helps organizations grow their analytics maturity: Google Cloud Platform (GCP). GCP is Google's suite of cloud computing products, including storage, computing, networking, and machine learning services. Indeed, Forrester Research named Google Cloud a Leader in Data Management for Analytics.[17]

Leveraging cloud computing increases the pace at which an organization can make decisions, adapt, and innovate—a chief indicator that an organization has reached the run phase in its journey. The purpose, platforms, people, and processes that we've discussed thus far all work together to prepare us for this vital step.

---

17 "Forrester Research names Google Cloud a Leader in Data Management for Analytics," Google Cloud, 2020, https://cloud.google.com/forrester-data-management-analytics.

Why have we worked so hard to get here? Because greater analytics maturity can alleviate marketing pain points, promote better business outcomes, and drive a greater payoff.

Note: For the second edition of this book, we have added a new section on Google Ads Data Hub, which can be found toward the end of the chapter.

MARKETING PAIN POINTS

While Google Cloud Platform was designed to solve many problems, some of its services are uniquely positioned to help companies navigate the constantly evolving marketing world. In order to break down how Google Cloud can extend your marketing capabilities, we first need to understand the problems that marketing technology is currently facing.

One of the most common pain points for today's marketer is disparate data. There are so many available solutions for SEO, analytics, CRM, email marketing, and paid advertising that getting a complete picture of your data can be a daunting task. Two problems make getting a big-picture view particularly challenging.

First, where can you store all of this data together? Marketing teams need a way to store data cheaply and efficiently where it's consumable, but they often lack engineering resources.

Second, marketing teams need a system that connects data seamlessly so it can be viewed and consumed outside of the daunting manual upload process.

Even if they overcome these challenges and start gathering the data, today's marketers face a third major challenge in trying to find actionable insights from that data. One way this can be done is through the use of aggregate and interactive dashboarding. Google Cloud Platform has direct integrations with Data Studio. However, Google Cloud Platform also has a suite of machine learning and data exploration tools that make advanced analysis much easier.

Finally, how are you going to activate this data? Once this sea of data is collected, integrated, and analyzed, the question becomes: what is next? How do you take the results of the models and the analysis and activate these insights?

DATA STORAGE

Google Cloud Platform offers many data storage solutions, but our main focus will be Cloud Storage, BigQuery, and BigTable. When evaluating the strengths of these services, we will look at cost, efficiency, and purpose.

Cloud Storage's purpose is file storage. It operates just like a folder on your computer, except it can be shared, exposed, and managed all within the cloud. When building an automated data pipeline in the cloud, Cloud Storage can be used as the entry point or intermediary as you consume files and push them into your data lake (a data lake being a vast, undefined pool of raw data). Cloud Storage is extremely cheap to use and even has built-in policies for removing old, unused data. In a sense, it serves as the glue that connects GCP services together.

BigQuery is by far the most popular Google Cloud Platform storage solution due largely to its efficiency of time and value. At the time of this writing, it costs only $0.02 per GB to store data in BigQuery, with that cost lowering even further the longer the data stays in the platform.

BigQuery was designed to cheaply store mass amounts of data while giving the user the power to query very large datasets as if it were a small database. This makes it the perfect solution for building a data lake or data warehouse. BigQuery autointegrates with platforms like Data Studio and Google Analytics, making it much easier to bring data together and display it. Using a platform like BigQuery to combine all marketing data sources allows for a single view of marketing efforts while maintaining low cost and high visibility. Combining marketing data in BigQuery is also a first step toward creating models for advanced analysis.

BigTable was designed for analysis. Structurally, it operates similarly to BigQuery, but it is much faster. While BigQuery is designed for very large queries and executes quite fast, sometimes it can take thirty seconds or more to respond to a query, so if you need to display the results quickly, you will want a faster solution. While it is significantly more expensive than BigQuery, it offers increased processing, giving much quicker response times. If you are building an analysis system to be consumed by the public, BigTable is a great solution to consider.

ETL

ETL stands for extract, transform, and load, which means data needs to be pulled, put into a usable format, and then pushed to a database where it can be consumed. ETL engineers help set up data pipelines that allow data to flow continuously, which allows for agile marketing decisions.

Ideally, your marketing platform will autoconnect to BigQuery,[18] but sometimes you need an engineer to write software that will connect to both your marketing APIs and BigQuery or Cloud Storage. You may also need a DevOps engineer to set up a server so the script can run every day. Google Cloud Platform offers ETL solutions that aim to take the DevOps out of ETL and keep the engineering as simple as possible.

Often, when first extracting data from a platform, it starts as a software script which then needs to be hosted on a server and run every day. These small scripts inspired Google to develop Cloud Functions, a service that hosts and runs a single script as long as its execution time is under ten minutes. The beauty of Cloud Functions is that it removes DevOps from the equation. It also connects to BigQuery and can be scheduled to repeat. To start ETL processes, an engineer simply has to write the scripts to connect the platforms. Cloud Functions is very cheap, costing less than one cent per run.

Unfortunately, some ETL problems are too large for Cloud Functions, need more processing, run longer than ten minutes, or are simply too complex for a single script. For larger, more sophisticated data pipelines, Google has developed Dataflow. One large feature advantage of Dataflow is that it supports streaming data as well as batch data. Streaming processing allows data to flow even faster into your data lake, so marketers can respond faster. Dataflow also solves scaling problems since it is designed to scale alongside your data.

DATA ANALYSIS

Once you solve the first and second pain points of bringing

---

18   "Analytics 360 and BigQuery: The Power of Connection," Analytics 360 Feature Brief, 2018, https://services.google.com/fh/files/misc/analytics_360_bigquery_integration_feature_brief.pdf.

your data together, you can then focus on the third: finding the real value in that data. Google Cloud Platform provides a suite of prebuilt tools that make finding insights in your data much simpler. Among those tools are Cloud AI, Cloud Dataprep, as well as a few prebuilt machine learning apps.

CLOUD DATAPREP

Finding insights in your marketing data isn't always obvious. Cloud Dataprep is designed to help you visualize, interact, and analyze data in the cloud without having to become a data scientist. It takes the software out of data transformation and allows your team to discover insights without the need for a whole analytics team.

CLOUD AUTOML

AutoML is Google's suite of prebuilt machine learning models, focusing on three distinct areas: sight, language, and structure data. The sight APIs are designed to help characterize different visuals from your photo or video assets, including YouTube videos, advertising creatives, banners on your website, and much more. While you've probably already collected data on which visuals are outperforming others, with AutoML's sight products, you can begin to understand why they are outperforming other visuals.

Of course, a major aspect of marketing creatives is the messaging they contain. Much like visuals, AutoML allows you to classify the text associated with your marketing assets to understand why some text might be performing better than others. AutoML's language services offer both translation services and natural language assessment. For marketing purposes, the natural language service can be used to identify the attitude and sentiment of your text to find out how your campaigns are being received by your customers, which will help you develop the perfect voice.

Recommendations API is a machine learning product available in Google Cloud Platform that helps you discover patterns in shopping behavior, altering your products in a way that best fits you. The platform suggests the best products to pair together, the best assortment on a webpage, and even makes pricing suggestions. It's a perfect way to optimize your e-commerce experience without expensive data science resources.

CLOUD AI

The beauty of AutoML's prebuilt models is that they eliminate the need for a full data science team. You can gain machine learning insights with minimal engineering efforts. However, if you already have a full data science team and are ready for the run phase of your analytics maturity, Cloud AI might be the better solution for you.

Cloud AI helps your data science team by making the typical data science pipeline much easier. It can take a lot of resources to create a model, create an automated pipeline for applying that model, and then find a good place to store the model. Cloud AI brings all of these concepts to the cloud, making them simpler and cheaper.

Now that we've covered the services within Google Cloud Platform that can help marketing projects, let's explore how they work together to create a faster pace and greater payoff. We'll dive deep to discover three ways your organization can utilize

Google Cloud for marketing: customer lifetime value (CLV), propensity modeling, and forecasting.

CUSTOMER LIFETIME VALUE AND CUSTOMER-CENTRICITY

Customer lifetime value (CLV) is a metric used by marketers to measure the overall value of a customer's relationship with a brand or company. Unlike lifetime spend or lifetime orders, which are straightforward metrics used to summarize customers' transaction histories, customer lifetime value reflects both past and future purchasing behaviors. Using CLV as a key performance indicator is a natural fit for companies with a customer-centric marketing strategy.

Not all customers are created equal, so companies that use the insights provided by CLV gain a competitive advantage. By aligning the development and delivery of products and services with the current and future needs of your highest value customers, you can maximize your customers' long-term financial value.[19]

Customer-centricity shifts the focus from short-term goals, like driving the next conversion, to long-term goals, such as designing the optimal customer experience for your very best customers. In order to execute a customer-centric strategy, however, the first step is to identify your best customers. That's where CLV comes in, providing a means of valuing and ranking customers based on both their past and future purchases, which is essential to any customer-centric strategy.

19   Peter Fader, Customer Centricity: Focus on the Right Customers for Strategic Advantage (Philadelphia, PA: Wharton School Press, 2012).

STRATEGIC ADVANTAGE MODELING WITH CLV

There are several different approaches to calculating CLV, ranging from a simple formula to complex machine learning methods. For companies that are new to CLV, we recommend starting with the probabilistic models developed by Peter Fader and Bruce Hardie. The most popular is the Pareto/Negative Binomial Distribution Model (PNBD), which is used to model noncontractual relationships with customers where transactions can occur at any time. Similar models exist for modeling contractual settings, such as subscriptions, or discrete purchasing opportunities like annual events.[20]

Regardless of which one you use, the model is fit to your company's historical data. The PNBD models the purchase propensity of each customer (how many future purchases they will make) and their churn risk (the probability they have already ceased being a customer). The predictions from the PNBD model are combined with a model of their spending habits and then discounted to present value. Predicted CLV is the sum of the present values of projected future cash flows.

Let's look at a hypothetical example:

A company has two customers, Kevin and Hilary. Kevin has spent $575 throughout his relationship with the company, and Hilary has spent $525. As both customers have spent between $500 and $600, they look similar at first glance and would likely be treated similarly by the company in terms of loyalty programs, campaigns, and targeting. However, based on the signals inherent to their particular purchase histories, Kevin has much greater potential to drive future value for the company.

---

20 Peter S. Fader and Bruce G.S. Hardie, "Simple Probability Models for Computing CLV and CE," *Handbook of Research on Customer Equity in Marketing* (January 2015): 77-100.

He is more likely to be an active customer (has not churned), and he is predicted to make more purchases and spend more on each future purchase. Despite their initial similarity, it's clear that Kevin is the higher value customer to the company, so a customer-centric strategy would prioritize Kevin's needs over Hilary's. Without CLV modeling, it would be very difficult to detect these signals in their respective behaviors.

Sample Customer Lifetime Value Report

Customer	Historical Spend	Predicted Churn Risk	Predicted Future Transactions	Predicted CLV
Kevin	$575	35%	2.4	$858
Hilary	$525	70%	0.8	$558

© InfoTrust

CLV IN ACTION

As shown in the example above, once you've calculated customer lifetime value, you can rank your customers and make appropriate strategic decisions. Who are your most valuable and loyal customers? Who are your low-value or at-risk customers? Which customers are in-between?

To drive retention and long-term success, nurture your high-value group. They are the backbone of your company, and you can afford to target them with more expensive forms of media to keep them engaged. Offer loyalty programs to make them feel appreciated. Understand their current and future needs and optimize your customer experience accordingly. They are worth the extra investment and attention because of their outsized influence on the bottom line.

For medium-value customers or those with a moderate churn risk, you have the opportunity to make a real impact. Some of these customers may not be convinced of your product's or service's value, so how can you personalize your messaging to highlight your unique value proposition?

Others may be highly motivated by discounts and promotions, so which special campaigns can you target to them that you would not offer to the entire customer base? Maybe your company is simply not top of mind with some of these customers, so how can you tailor your campaigns to reach them at the right time with the right messaging?

As you narrow your focus on the needs of your highest-value customers, apply what you learn to the medium-value group: which experiences or categories propelled customers to become high value? How can you replicate that with your current medium-value group? If the retention rate of the medium-value group is 50 percent, and you boost retention to 60 percent through your marketing efforts, you will have made a substantial impact on your customer base. Don't neglect the middle group because you have a great opportunity to impact the bottom line by improving the outcomes of these customers.

In reality, the majority of your customers will be considered low value. While some of these customers might surprise you, the overall retention rate for this group is usually quite low. Many of them have probably already churned, and others are new customers who have little available data, which makes their signals weak.

Due to the high degree of uncertainty with these customers, you should choose your campaigns carefully. Avoid expensive campaigns because you're unlikely to see a positive ROI. However, don't ignore these customers entirely. Set realistic expectations for low-value customers—only a fraction of them will return to make another purchase based on your marketing—and keep your focus on optimizing for the highest-value customers.

GETTING STARTED WITH CLV ON GOOGLE CLOUD PLATFORM

Although there are many ways to run CLV models, one key benefit of using the PNBD model is that it has a low barrier to entry. To create your dataset, you need a customer-level transaction log that includes the dates when purchases were made and the amount spent on each.[21] Collect data going back at least eight to ten purchase cycles, so the model has enough historical data to learn from. Those three columns (customer ID, date, spend) are all you need to predict CLV using the PNBD model.[22]

Although it's often possible to run CLV models locally on your computer, we recommend using Google Cloud Platform's computing resources. GCP autoscales to provide the right amount of resources for your model, and you can automate the models to run on a daily or weekly basis. With the models running regularly, you always have up-to-date data that you can use for targeting your campaigns.

We also advise pushing the CLV predictions to Google Analytics so remarketing audiences can be built and shared with other products in Google Marketing Platform, such as Google Ads and Display & Video. This allows you to tailor your campaigns

---

21 If you want more flexibility or to incorporate other data, you'll need to choose a more sophisticated model, such as a deep neural network.

22 With any modeling project, don't forget to review and validate the assumptions of the model. Most models are designed to be used under specific conditions, so it's important to confirm that your real-world data is consistent with those assumptions. If your data is fundamentally different from the data the model was designed to analyze, the model results will be inaccurate.

to your different customer groups and expand the reach of your current campaigns by creating similar audiences.[23]

Here is an example of how to utilize Google Cloud Platform for CLV:

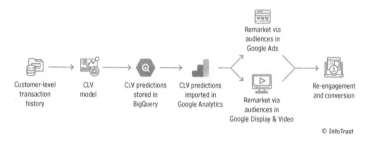

Customer Lifetime Value Model

© InfoTrust

CLV is a powerful metric for marketers. As the bedrock of a customer-centric strategy, it enables you to value and rank your customers based on their long-term value to the company. Running your CLV models on Google Cloud Platform and pushing the results into Google Analytics gives you the tools to activate customer-centric strategies using audience targeting.

PROPENSITY MODELING

Another marketing use case that contributes to audience creation and strategy is propensity modeling. Like CLV, a propensity model detects signals in users' behavior and uses those signals to make predictions about what they will do in the future.

---

23 Similar audiences are machine learning-powered audiences created by Google based on an existing audience, such as high-value customers. Google uses machine learning to understand what these customers have in common and then identifies new users who are similar. Similar audiences help you grow your customer base by targeting ads to users who resemble your highest valued customers but are unfamiliar with your company. "About similar audiences on the Display Network," Google Ads Help, accessed March 3, 2020, https://support.google.com/google-ads/answer/2676774?hl=en.

However, while CLV is designed to predict the holistic value a customer provides to your company, propensity modeling is typically used to make predictions over a shorter time frame.

CLV is valuable because it's an essential part of a larger, comprehensive customer-centric strategy. Propensity modeling, on the other hand, has a narrower focus: improving the ROI of remarketing campaigns.

Propensity models are typically used to predict which customers will purchase over the next three, seven, fourteen, or thirty days, but you can design the model to use any time horizon that makes sense for your company. You can also use the model to predict if a specific product or category will be purchased. The output of the model is a score ranging from zero to one, which you can interpret as a probability. Scores close to zero indicate that a customer is unlikely to purchase, while scores close to one suggest that the customer has a high probability of purchasing during the selected time period. You can incorporate these scores into your remarketing audiences to target individuals during the final consideration phase of their customer journey.

There are many different models you can use for propensity modeling. We recommend getting started with a logistic regression model, but you could also use decision tree or neural network-based methods. Though you can get started with CLV modeling using just three columns of data, we don't recommend that for propensity modeling. Instead, it's best to build a detailed dataset that includes many measures of customer behavior, such as which products they viewed and which content they clicked, watched, and shared.

Propensity models typically perform better when they are fit to a broad dataset of customer behaviors, so integrating with data from your CRM and advertising platforms often improves the accuracy of the predictions. The goal is to give the model all of the relevant indicators that a customer has reached the final consideration phase of the purchase cycle, so you can target them at the right time to reduce the number of lost sales.

Because propensity modeling is focused on a short time frame, the models are most actionable when they are run regularly. Accordingly, we recommend using Google Cloud Platform for building and deploying the models so they can run as often as necessary. Every time the model runs, the predictions (scores) are stored in a BigQuery table. The scores are then imported into Google Analytics so they can be used to create the remarketing audiences, which are shared with the other products within GMP.

Here is an example of a typical propensity modeling architecture on GCP:

Propensity Model

Customer behavior data from Google Analytics

Customer data from CRM, CDP, or other marketing platform

CLV model

CLV predictions stored in BigQuery

CLV predictions imported in Google Analytics

Remarket via audiences in Google Ads

Remarket via audiences in Google Display & Video

Re-engagement and conversion

© InfoTrust

Propensity modeling is a practical and effective way to improve the ROI of remarketing campaigns. By leveraging the data from your analytics and advertising platforms, you can build models to uncover the signals in your customers' behavior that suggest they are in the final consideration phase of the purchase cycle. When you use Google Cloud Platform to run the models regularly and push up-to-date scores to GMP, you enable the marketing team to reach customers at the right time with the right messaging.

FORECASTING

Forecasting is the process of making predictions using data collected at regular intervals over time. If you want to make predictions using metrics that you collect every week, every day, every hour, every minute, or every second, statistical forecasting models are the right choice. We recommend getting started with the Holt-Winters model or the class of models known as autoregressive integrated moving average (ARIMA).

Forecasting is used to solve several different types of problems and can be valuable for many types of companies. For websites or apps that generate revenue by selling advertising space, such as publishers and online games, using a forecasting model to predict page views or screen views can help them understand their upcoming available ad inventory.

For e-commerce retailers, forecasting the demand for their products helps with production planning, inventory management, and marketing campaign strategy. For example, many of our clients run a number of major promotions throughout the year, particularly during holiday seasons, that are extremely important to their annual financial performance. Their marketing strategies for these promotions can make or break their overall performance for the year.

We built forecasting models for one client who was struggling with a lack of visibility into future sales and campaign performance. They wanted to know if their campaigns were working without waiting hours for standard reporting. Above all, they wanted to know if they were on track to meet their sales targets and, if not, which channels were off track. With this information, their channel managers could then spring into action, adjusting their campaigns midstream to avoid a disaster.

A few key ingredients are required in order to run forecasting models on Google Cloud Platform.

First, you need a data collection process. To make predictions about the near future, models use data from the recent past. The frequency of your data collection process depends on the frequency of your model (hourly, daily, weekly). The data collection process we designed uses Cloud Functions to gather data and stores it in BigQuery.

Second, you need to pass the data through the model so that it generates forecasts. Again, we used Cloud Functions to perform these operations and BigQuery to store the forecasts.

Third, you need a data visualization tool, like Data Studio, to display the forecasted data and make it easy to share within the organization.

Marketers crave the level of visibility that forecasting can provide. It reveals if they're on track to meet important sales targets. Often, clients come to us because their marketing plan doesn't deliver the results they need, so they want to pivot. Forecasting allows them to pivot sooner so they can adjust their strategies in the middle of a campaign rather than waiting until the campaign is over to discover that they underperformed.

Forecasting Model

Data collection process → Forecasting model → Forecasts stored in BigQuery → Dashboard created in Data Studio

© InfoTrust

ADS DATA HUB

We are entering a privacy-centric world where users expect, and demand, to own and control their data. As a result, data clean rooms have become increasingly popular. A data clean room is a secure location where large companies such as Google, Facebook, or Amazon house user-level advertising data. Data clean rooms are privacy-centric and only allow aggregated data to be pulled from the platform. Google's version of this is called Ads Data Hub (ADH).[24]

For companies that use Google's advertising platforms—Display & Video 360, YouTube, Google Ads, and so on—ADH is a place where Google shares event-level data in a way that maintains user privacy. Event-level data includes impressions, viewability metrics, geo-location, device type, and additional event-specific data points. Currently, this kind of data is present in its Campaign Manager data transfer service, a service that allows you to transfer advertising data from Campaign Manager or Display & Video 360 to BigQuery on a schedule.

Once your reporting data is in BigQuery, you can run queries to analyze and review the data. In March of 2021, Google will fully redact all user IDs from the data transfer service. At that point,

---

24   Ariel Opelt, "Introduction to Ads Data Hub," InfoTrust, November 19, 2020, https://infotrust.com/articles/introduction-to-ads-data-hub/.

the user ID will only be available in the Ads Data Hub clean room—advertisers will not be able to see the user ID themselves.

With ADH, not only can you see how users are interacting with ads down to the impression, but you can combine the data with other platforms in Google Cloud for some powerful analysis.

HOW DOES ADH WORK?

Ads Data Hub is a Google-owned BigQuery project. Advertisers do not have direct access to event-level data but must run queries to analyze their advertising data through ADH. To do that, the organization will have to create its own project in BigQuery. In other words, there will be two BigQuery projects—one belonging to Google and one belonging to your company—that are connected in the ADH interface.

This gives you access to your event-level advertising data, but it also protects *your* company data from being accessed by Google. ADH does not store any data; all query output is stored in your company-owned BigQuery project. Only the queries cross between the two. This enables Google to maintain privacy for individuals, while you can protect your own internal data at the same time.

Once ADH and your company's BigQuery project are integrated, you will need to ensure that there is a common ID in both places. The best way to do this is through Floodlight, the conversion-tracking system for Google's advertising platforms. Floodlights are placed on your website to track important user interactions such as purchases, "add to cart," newsletter sign-ups, and so on. Inside the Floodlight, you can create custom variables that track additional information about user interaction. It's important to use an ID such as account ID, customer ID, or the Google client ID as a custom variable in your Floodlights.

For organizations interested in connecting ADH and their first-party data from Google Analytics or their CRM, the ID or IDs selected should be present on all platforms. That ID will become the common ID between the Google advertising platform, your website, and your CRM, so you can examine and analyze data between all three using ADH. To learn more about Google's advertising platforms, see chapter four: "Google Marketing Platform."

ADH IN ACTION

Ads Data Hub has a number of features and benefits, depending on what you are looking for. While you can join ADH with first-party data, it isn't a requirement. ADH holds all your advertising data, which opens a number of analysis, audience creation, and attribution options, both with and without first-party data. Let's look at some examples of what you can do with ADH.

ANALYSIS

ADH unlocks all sorts of new capabilities for analysis, so you can more clearly understand who your users are and customize your remarketing and advertising accordingly. Advertisers can run analyses to understand how many users overlap between two or more audiences. Understanding audience overlap could mean that some customers are overexposed to your campaigns. Finding users who overlap could mean it's time to refine which audiences are being used for each campaign.

ADH also allows companies to understand how often users are

being exposed to their ad campaigns. Understanding campaign frequency can help reduce advertising spend by not showing more ads than are necessary to a specific user. Frequency analysis helps companies understand what an ideal advertising frequency is for the specific audiences and campaigns they are targeting.

ADH also offers the ability to learn more about how users respond to your video display campaigns, as well as the viewability of these campaigns. Plus, ADH can help analyze the percentage completed of video ads, such as TrueView in-stream ads. Understanding where users stop watching a video helps media teams review what's happening during that time. This information can then be shared with the media or creative teams to help enhance future campaigns.

ADH can also be joined with first-party data such as Google Analytics or your CRM. Combining multiple platforms in this manner allows businesses to further the analysis being run. Evaluating ad frequency could be enhanced by joining additional key performance indicators (KPI) such as registering for your website or completing an offline purchase. With this data, you can understand the best ad frequency to help encourage users to register or complete an offline purchase.

AUDIENCE CREATION

After analyzing the data within ADH or joining ADH with your first-party data, you can start to build targeted audiences. You might notice that many users overlap between two of the main audiences you target. Let's discuss how to build unique audiences using this new knowledge.

Start by identifying the high, medium, and low engagement

users. You'll need to define what each segment means for your business. High engagement might mean users who engaged with three or more ads and have previously converted on your website. Medium engagement users could be people who view at least two ads and have previously been to your website. Low engagement users could be users who view at least two ads but never click through to your website. Using ADH and potentially first-party data, you can now build an audience for each of these user segments.

When building audiences, remember to build both an *include* and *exclude* audience. Excluding users from an audience isn't always common practice but it helps reduce audience overlap and narrows who is exposed to your ads. For example, if you choose to run a YouTube brand awareness campaign, it's not necessary to expose the high engagement audience. These are individuals who are already familiar with your brand and are likely to convert. Instead, create a targeted campaign specifically for these users and exclude them from a brand awareness campaign.

While analysis output is sent to BigQuery, audiences built in ADH are sent directly to Google Ads or Display &Video 360. No additional integration work is required.

ATTRIBUTION

Understanding the customer journey is always a challenge for businesses. ADH opens the door to allow businesses to understand the advertising journey for their customers. With ADH, advertisers no longer have to focus on using last-click or first-click attribution. In these two attribution models, 100 percent of the conversion credit is given to the last or first advertising interaction, respectively.

Attribution models that give 100 percent of the conversion value to one interaction (last or first click) don't provide insights into how (or if) other touchpoints helped users during the journey. Focusing on them can bias specific advertising campaigns. For example, in last-click attribution models, brand awareness campaigns will almost never receive credit for the conversion.

Instead, companies should look to more data-driven attribution models that allow companies to understand how each touchpoint in a user's advertising journey should be credited. Shapley and Markov attribution models are two mathematical algorithms used to estimate the contribution that each touchpoint had on the conversion, which you can use to assign partial credit for the overall conversion. Both Shapley[25] and Markov[26] attribution models are available within ADH.

Let's examine how these two attribution models work within ADH. Let's suppose your business has several campaigns running that span YouTube and Display & Video 360. You've configured a brand awareness campaign, a content campaign for users who viewed a specific section of your website, and a campaign to reengage users who have not visited your website in ten days.

A single user views all three campaigns in order, and after seeing the reengagement campaign, they arrive on the website. Traditionally, you cannot assign credit to all three channels based on their level of contribution to the conversion. Using Shapley or Markov attribution, you can understand how each campaign should be credited for the overall customer conversion. Instead

25 "Shapley Value Analysis," Ads Data Hub, accessed December 28, 2020, https://developers.google.com/ads-data-hub/guides/shapley.

26 "Markov Chain Analysis," Ads Data Hub, accessed December 28, 2020, https://developers.google.com/ads-data-hub/guides/markov.

of saying the reengagement campaign gets 100 percent credit, you may find that the content campaign deserves 50 percent of the credit for the conversion.

As we mentioned, ADH can also be combined with first-party data such as Google Analytics 4 or your CRM. Adding in this additional dataset can make your attribution more sophisticated. Joining with your first-party data, you can understand how to attribute credit from impression to conversion and all the touchpoints in between. This attribution credit allows you to better spend your money and team resources. Now, instead of only focusing on the reengagement campaign, resources can be shifted to enhancing the content campaign.

Whether you are running an analysis or trying to understand the best attribution model, Google's Ads Data Hub will export all query results to your company-owned BigQuery project. Data in BigQuery can be connected to visualization platforms such as Data Studio or Looker to help illustrate what the data is showing. Consider using a visualization tool when communicating ADH findings with other team members and departments.

REASONS TO ADOPT ADH

Although ADH is not a new product, many organizations haven't yet wrapped their heads around how Ads Data Hub works. GDPR, CCPA, and other privacy laws (see chapter three for more details) have required companies to protect and secure user data. ADH offers a controlled environment where advertisers can access this data while the data clean room controls the privacy regulations. Companies should start testing data clean rooms to understand what information is present and how to utilize the data to its fullest potential.

Beyond this, there are a few distinct reasons why we believe organizations should use Ads Data Hub. ADH offers native integration with Google Ads, YouTube, Campaign Manager, and Display & Video 360. This integration makes it easy to get started and easy to share audiences back to these platforms. At the time of this writing, ADH does not support Search Ads 360 or Search for Google Ads. However, Search is expected to be available for ADH in the coming year.

ADH is very privacy-focused. For this reason, Google runs three separate checks on all ADH queries. The first is a static check that looks at what is contained in the query, so Google can ensure a business isn't trying to pull any user identifiers. The second is an aggregation requirement. ADH will only aggregate data of fifty or more users, so you won't get results for your query if there are fewer than that. Unfortunately, this means you can't do granular searches. For a large organization, this shouldn't be a problem, but smaller organizations might find it frustrating.

The third and final check is a difference check. ADH looks at past queries your company has run and compares them to your current query to make sure you're not trying to compare results at an individual user level. The difference check looks at a previous query you've run, such as a YouTube video campaign placement, by domain, gender, and device. It then compares the output from that query with the current query you are running—your YouTube video campaign placement—by domain, geolocation, and device. In this instance, Google's ADH results might remove some rows from the output that is sent to BigQuery in order to prevent your business from identifying any user-level data.

SHOULD YOU MOVE TO ADH?

In our opinion, any business currently using Google's data transfer service should move to Ads Data Hub, especially since user ID will be redacted in early 2021. As user ID becomes redacted, companies who transferred data to a local data lake for advanced modeling will be missing the information needed to build this model at the user level. In order to build local data models, user journeys, or attribution models, you would need a user ID, but moving forward, organizations will only be able to access user IDs in a privacy-focused way, such as through Ads Data Hub.

Any organization that is advertising on Google will benefit from ADH because they will gain a more complete picture of their data, breaking down silos to get a better sense of the customer journey from impression to conversion.

DATA ACTIVATION WITH GOOGLE MARKETING PLATFORM

In the summer of 2020, after we finished the first edition of this book, Forrester released a thought leadership paper commissioned by Google. Survey results revealed that 84 percent of respondents believe predictive analytics is *critical* or *very important*, 81 percent believe that machine learning and automated insights are *critical* or *very important*, and 84 percent believe media activation is *critical* or *very important*.[27]

Since you are already familiar with Google Marketing Platform from chapter four, we thought it would be a good idea to provide some examples of how insights produced through different

---

27 "The Future of Analytics," *Forrester Consulting*, July 2020, https://marketingplatform.google.com/about/resources/the-future-of-analytics/.

types of modeling on Google Cloud Platform can be integrated through Google Marketing Platform with different upstream systems to achieve immediate business results.

Before we jump into examples, here is a brief reminder of how the data flows:

DATA FLOW ONE

1. Export data from Analytics 360 into BigQuery.
2. Once your model is built, additional data elements (such as a lifetime value prediction) can be associated with your data records in BigQuery.
3. Use API to export data from BigQuery and Analytics Data Import to update customer data originally stored in Analytics 360.
4. As a result, your Analytics 360 data will be enhanced with Cloud-produced insights.

Remember, Analytics 360 has native integration with systems such as Display & Video 360, Optimize 360, Surveys 360, and so on.

DATA FLOW TWO

1. Bring your offline conversions from BigQuery into Campaign Manager 360 through the Campaign Manager 360 API.
2. Share conversions with Display & Video 360 and Search Ads 360 so your campaign bidding strategies can optimize for those types of events.

DATA FLOW THREE

1. Analytics 360 can be integrated with the Salesforce Marketing Cloud (as covered in chapter four).
2. This integration allows the marketer to take an audience into Analytics 360 and, using new insights generated in BigQuery, launch an email marketing campaign in the Salesforce Marketing Cloud.

Here are some examples of audiences you may want to build as a result of your analyses:

- Create an audience of high-value customers and share this audience with Display & Video, Google Ads, and Search Ads 360.
- Create an audience made up of customers you want to share a discount with, then customize your website for the audience in Optimize 360.
- Create an audience made up of customers who have low-revenue prediction or high-churn probability and find out why with Surveys 360.
- Reach audiences with high-churn probability in Salesforce Marketing Cloud to send them a special deal.

BUILDING YOUR CLOUD FOR MARKETING TEAM

Getting the most out of Cloud for Marketing requires having the right kinds of people on your team.

First, you need a database architect who understands how your data moves through your platforms, where it is at any particular moment, and how your individual pieces of data speak to each other.

Second, you need a data engineer whose job is to bring order to your data and prepare it for specific purposes. The engineer makes sure all data is stored properly for ease of access and pulls out the appropriate data when it's needed.

Third, you need a data scientist who can take the specific data provided by your engineer and begin the modeling process. Your data scientist will work with your data engineer to figure out where to store the outcomes in order to provide feedback. Once feedback loops are in place, you need a data analyst who can translate your outcomes into practical information that company leaders will understand. Your data analyst doesn't have to know how to build the models.

You might also consider having a cloud architect on your team. This is the individual responsible for figuring out how to use different cloud services. While your database architect focuses on your data, the cloud architect stays informed on various cloud-related products and figures out how they fit together.

Depending on the size of your company, one person for each of these roles should be enough—four or five people working together to acquire, sort, model, and analyze data. Your data scientist and analyst might be outside consultants, or they can be in-house members of your team. Either way, you need those roles in place to make the most of your data.

It's also a good idea to get your marketing teams involved because they are the ones who will end up changing their strategies based on the outcome of these models. The results of the models can only move the business forward when the marketing team puts them to use.

PART THREE

GET WHERE YOU NEED TO BE

Now that we've looked at the main components of digital analytics, such as data governance, Google Marketing Platform, and Google Cloud, we will walk you through the stages of digital analytics maturity within specific types of organizations. You'll see how all of these pieces fit together, along with the 6 Ps, in different industries. After all, the way a newspaper such as *The Washington Post* achieves analytics maturity will differ quite a bit from a packaged-goods company.

We have chosen three common verticals that we often work with, breaking them down to reveal how the 6 Ps, along with the components of digital analytics, come together as they journey toward multi-moment maturity. As you read through these chapters, consider where you are in your own organization, and think about the tools that you will need to get to the next stage of maturity.

CHAPTER EIGHT

DIGITAL ANALYTICS MATURITY: NEWS AND MEDIA ORGANIZATIONS

CHAPTER CONTRIBUTOR: ANDY GIBSON

 Andy Gibson is Head of Vertical: News & Media at InfoTrust. He has many years of experience working with some of the largest news, media, and publishing companies in the world to improve their digital analytics capabilities, and he has delivered hundreds of trainings on Google Marketing Platform and its products.

Andy is also an adjunct instructor at the University of Cincinnati's Lindner College of Business, where he teaches a graduate-level course on digital analytics with his colleague, Pam Castricone, who is also a contributor to this book.

Outside of work, Andy enjoys reading, dogs, and the University of Dayton Flyers basketball.

In the previous chapter, we examined the four stages of digital analytics maturity, looking at specific actions that help organizations grow from nascent all the way to multi-moment. However, the truth is, this journey through analytics maturity looks quite different depending on your industry. In the next few chapters, we want to focus on specific industries, giving you a look at how the four stages of maturity play out in these spaces.

We will begin by examining news and media organizations (often referred to as "publishers"). As we examine the stages of maturity for these organizations, consider the impact of progress on the 6 Ps, particularly the capacity of people within the organization and the need for changing processes.

NASCENT PUBLISHERS: LACK OF FIRST-PARTY DATA

In our experience, many news and media organizations are still in the nascent stage. They tend to use analytics at a more basic level with a focus on overall site traffic and content metrics. There are a couple of reasons for this.

First, their advertising revenue is still based largely on impressions and clicks on their website and apps. Therefore, their KPIs mostly consist of high-level traffic metrics like page views, sessions, and users since those are closely tied to impressions and clicks. They might also drive user engagement across the platforms to generate additional advertising revenue. Bear in mind, subscriptions are a separate revenue stream that can be the focus for a publisher like *The New York Times*. Ultimately, the business model drives the KPIs for a publisher.

Second, their audiences tend to be largely anonymous; they often don't have a direct relationship with site or app visitors, depending on the company's business model. Publishers without subscription models generally have a much larger anonymous audience than publishers with a subscription model.

Let's walk through an example: Think about your local TV station. It's generally owned by a large news and media publisher that also owns many other local TV stations across the country. This station will most likely have OTT (over-the-top) apps that allow the content to be viewed on platforms like Roku, Apple TV, or Fire TV. These OTT apps are in addition to a website and mobile apps for each station.

Often, there is no subscription model for a local TV channel since it's managed by a cable TV provider, like DirecTV or YouTube TV. This means the users who come to the local TV station's content remain largely anonymous. If you've ever tried to watch live local TV online, you know you have to sign in to your cable provider's account. Generally, that login information isn't shared with the local TV station or the news and media company that owns the TV station.

News and media companies that sell subscriptions online have a more direct, though still imperfect, relationship with their users. Think of a media organization like ESPN, which has cable TV channels, websites, along with mobile and OTT apps that include two streaming platforms:

1. **ESPN/WatchESPN:** Cable TV channels that can be watched online via the ESPN website or apps but require an existing cable TV subscription with ESPN from a provider. ESPN's

customers don't pay ESPN directly but the cable TV provider.

2. **ESPN+**: An online subscription-only model that has exclusive content and is not tied to a cable TV subscription. Customers pay ESPN directly.

For the first option, if you want to watch ESPN through the website or app, you need to log in using your cable TV account. The data doesn't go directly to ESPN—it belongs to the cable TV provider, who, in many cases, doesn't share that information with ESPN. Consequently, ESPN has a blind spot as it pertains to the end user watching content through their site or app. They don't have access to any cable TV subscription information on these customers.

The second option is much more beneficial to ESPN as they have a direct relationship with the customer. All of the first-party subscription data, like customer information, subscription length, lifetime revenue, customer lifetime value, and more, is owned and usable by ESPN.

This direct relationship with the customer is one huge benefit of the subscription model. When customers buy a print or digital subscription to *The New York Times*, they have to provide personal information, such as name, email address, payment, and billing information. On top of that, *The New York Times* asks online subscribers to customize their reading experience by selecting topics of interest and subscribing to newsletters on those topics. These provide data points that the publisher can match with individual subscribers to better understand their preferences and predict their engagement, churn, and customer lifetime value (CLV).

When 50 percent or more of an audience is anonymous, a media company winds up with a large amount of traffic that lacks defining characteristics. Consequently, the company will struggle with two areas:

1. Creating an engaging, personalized experience for visitors.
2. Building granular audiences for advertisers to target based on defining characteristics, like demographic and interest data.

This lack of first-party data has been common in the industry, so many publishers have relied heavily on third-party data management platforms (DMPs) to create audiences for their advertisers.

In turn, historically, advertisers who purchase space on media organization websites have generally lacked the ability to do sophisticated targeting. They've used high-level audiences, such as people visiting from certain geographic areas or visiting certain sections of websites or apps. At the same time, media companies have had no real incentive to collect additional first-party data because advertisers haven't asked for it.

However, advertiser demands are changing. In the last few years, they have begun to demand more specific targeting so they can reach more granular audiences, but third-party solutions, such as DMPs, can't always provide that data due to new browser initiatives such as Apple's ITP (Intelligent Tracking Prevention) which limits cookies.

DMPs are heavily reliant on browser cookies, so their efficacy moving forward is certainly in question. To meet advertiser demand, media organizations have no choice but to build comprehensive, scalable analytics architectures that collect more first-party audience data across their platforms. It's a significant but necessary undertaking, so publishers own their audience data, making them less reliant on third-party platforms that will be severely limited moving forward.

Generally, media organizations utilize a tag management system for data collection across their online platforms, and they use an ad distribution network like Google Ad Manager (formerly DoubleClick for Publishers or DFP) to show ads on their website and monetize audiences across their platforms. Depending on the publisher, they might also manage other marketing and analytics platforms like social media tools and email marketing systems.

They generally have a content management system (CMS) as the backbone of their content platforms, but these various platforms are rarely connected, and each one might be managed by a different team. The analytics team focuses on Analytics 360 or Adobe Analytics, while the social media team manages the social media platforms, and a separate email marketing team manages their newsletter subscriptions. The organization is filled with disparate, siloed data centers.

To be clear, this scenario isn't that different in the news and media industry as it is in other industries, but complicating the situation, media organizations also tend to operate in different markets, as with local TV stations. Furthermore, with a nascent publisher, each of those markets typically has its own team handling local data in local silos. Getting a holistic view of the audience is almost difficult, which is one reason why so many publishers without a defined audience and data strategy find themselves stuck in the nascent stage.

EMERGING PUBLISHERS: BETTER PERSONALIZED EXPERIENCES

Most publishers need to identify the drivers that will take them from the nascent stage to the emerging stage. In the current privacy climate, this has become more complicated. Publishers simply don't own much first-party data on their customers, so when they're trying to mature their analytics, they generally have to start with an audit.

We've worked with many media partners to help them with these audits, examining their analytics architecture to see what data they are currently collecting and what other first-party data points are necessary to collect. It's also important for the collected data to be unified across all of their platforms.

With improved first-party data, they can build better-personalized experiences for customers, but due to privacy regulations, collecting that data requires customer consent. Many media organizations lack a subscription model, so they don't have login capabilities. To get permission from customers to collect their data, they have to provide some kind of value exchange. A subscription (free or paid) is certainly an effective means of doing this as long as there is enough perceived value.

CONNECTED PUBLISHERS: UNIFIED FIRST-PARTY DATA

A media organization has entered the emerging stage once they have a scalable analytics architecture in place for collecting first-party data, as well as a strategy for acquiring that data. They might still have data siloed in a few different platforms, but they at least have a good setup to start collecting the data they need.

They're getting a better sense of how people engage with their content across platforms.

If they want to start targeting specific audiences or allow advertisers to engage those audiences, they need to start sharing their first-party data with other platforms. In Google Marketing Platform, this is easy because Analytics 360 has an integration with Google Ad Manager. Analytics 360 can generate audiences based on site behavior, and those audiences can then be shared to Google Ad Manager for advertisers to target. This provides a quick win for both publishers and advertisers.

Emerging media organizations need some kind of customer data platform (CDP), so they can unify their first-party data across their many platforms. In order to create a single customer view and grow beyond the emerging stage, all silos must be broken down. Information technology will need to be involved in integrating these various, disparate platforms and systems. To keep up, the IT team might have to take on a larger role across the organization.

As first-party data is brought together from these silos, some standardized processes will need to be created, and a point person identified within the organization who can communicate with all of the different teams: editorial, research, social media, ad monetization, email marketing, and so on. The point person and a set of standardized processes align these teams and help to create that holistic single-customer view.

MULTI-MOMENT PUBLISHERS: ACTIVATING UNIFIED CUSTOMER DATA

The final piece of the puzzle to become multi-moment is to

activate all of this unified customer data. Much of it can be done within the Google Cloud platform using products like BigQuery, which is integrated with Analytics 360 and many other Google Marketing Platform products. Because the organization can now create unified customer profiles that update on a continual basis based on specific user interactions across multiple platforms, they can start to activate this data in a number of ways.

Google Ad Manager has an integration with Analytics 360 that allows companies to create segments within Analytics 360 based on behavior, geographical data, or custom user data from other platforms, and send those audiences into Google Ad Manager for more granular targeting. This type of first-party data can also be activated through a content management system to deliver personalized experiences across all platforms.

For example, a newspaper website might be tracking each user's content preferences to understand what sections people visit most often. With that information, they can personalize their homepage based on each user's content preferences to deliver more engaging sessions.

They can also use A/B testing to further validate this personalized experience, learning what effect variables like position or size have on engagement. Optimize 360 is fully integrated with Analytics 360 and allows targeting and personalization based on specific engagement or characteristics.

If you want an example of a media organization providing an excellent, personalized digital experience, look at ESPN. When you create an account with ESPN, they ask for your favorite sports teams and, in turn, personalize your homepage with content that is relevant to those teams. I am an avid Dayton

Flyers basketball fan, so any upcoming Dayton games and team-related news will be prominently displayed on my ESPN homepage. They have my permission to acquire this data, and I gave it to them because they provide value in return through a personalized experience. It's their personalization and optimization that allow them to deliver more engaging experiences.

MOBILE AND OVER-THE-TOP (OTT) PLATFORMS

Most media organizations have been impacted by the rise of mobile, so the mobile customer experience is a more important part of the analytics strategy than ever before. The mobile app can't just look like a reskin of the website. Since media organizations tend to be video-heavy, over-the-top apps like Roku and Apple TV also play a major role.

Tracking for mobile apps and over-the-top platforms can be done through Analytics 360, applying the same methodologies as with other platforms, like understanding top stories and user engagement through video-centric tracking. Not only can Analytics 360 track which videos get the most views, but also how long people stay engaged. With articles, it can track how far down on the page they scroll, if they scroll at all. This reveals if users are reading the article, skimming it, or merely glancing at it before moving on to another page.

Engagement is important to any media organization. Typically, only a small percentage of video content or articles are being highly engaged with. Media organizations need to know what's working so they can create more of that specific type of content. In that way, engagement metrics provide a crucial guidepost for the creation of future content.

WHERE TO START?

When a media organization in the nascent stage approaches us looking to make fast progress moving through the maturity stages, we have a general plan of action that we put into place.

For the first sixty to ninety days, we recommend focusing internally on your company. Get to know all of the different teams collecting and using customer data and audit their processes to understand what data is and isn't being collected. Take note of any additional information that needs to be collected. You can't start building your analytics foundation until you have clarity on where your organization currently is.

For a company in the emerging stage, the first step is to audit your data architecture and ecosystem. Chances are, you're going to find siloed data throughout your organization, with different people in charge of different platforms and data points. This stage is also where you should incorporate the governance processes discussed in the first section. For media companies, the primary benefit of compliant data collection is complemented by a secondary benefit of improved performance once the platform architecture is optimized in a compliant state.

Leveraging our Tag Inspector platform, we often include a performance analysis in the Tag Governance Audit process. This allows organizations to quantify the performance and user experience impact of the tags loading on their sites. Given the often complex ad technology landscape on publishers' sites, there is a massive opportunity to consolidate the platforms in use, thereby removing large volumes of tags. In a recent engagement with a global media publisher, they were able to identify and remove roughly 20 percent of the unique ad tech platforms loading on a typical page as a result of the Governance Audit.

The result was a compliant data collection architecture and a noticeable improvement in page load times.

Unfortunately, the first step for many companies is to jump on the latest and greatest data platform, but if the prep work hasn't been done inside your organization, a flashy new platform might cause even more problems. Per our 6 Ps of Digital Transformation Model, get your internal people and processes in order before integrating new platforms.

MEASURING SUCCESS

As a media organization, once you start implementing changes to your digital analytics, you can measure success most effectively with a few KPIs. We recommend avoiding high-level KPIs like *traffic* because they don't guarantee success. Instead, success is best revealed by your ability to create more first-party customer data attributes, which lead to monetizing new, improved audiences and a more personalized visitor experience. As you move toward a single customer view, business value is driven by the activation of the first-party data being collected.

Let's suppose that in the beginning, you had three attributes for 1,000 customers, but now, through a shift in focus to first-party data collection and utilization, you have on average twenty attributes for those same customers. This is huge growth for the first-party data that can be activated. More user attributes provide your advertisers with more comprehensive information for audience targeting across your platforms, making the advertising more effective and, in turn, increasing the return on advertising spend (ROAS).

It's a competitive time for media organizations. Many have

begun using a subscription model to acquire and retain customers. Eventually, customers will tire of having so many subscriptions across different websites and apps, and we may see a move to a unified subscription model, similar to what Apple has tried to do with Apple News+.

However, Apple has struggled to get publishers on board due to issues like low subscription numbers, worries about losing control of the customer relationship, and concerns over Apple's share of the revenue.[28] Still, when you're competing with so many other media platforms and publishers, you have to hone your ability to provide a more targeted experience for users. The companies that do this well are thriving in the media space. Give people what they want to read, watch, or listen to, and give it to them in a way they enjoy, and they will keep coming back.

THE VALUE OF GOOGLE ANALYTICS 4 FOR NEWS & MEDIA

In October 2020, Google announced the next version of Google Analytics, called Google Analytics 4 (GA4), which offers a customer-centric measurement platform that was built with data governance and privacy in mind. GA4 will leverage Google's vast machine learning capabilities to surface insights automatically and create metrics and audiences that are predictive in nature.

GA4 presents an exciting opportunity for the news and media industry for a few reasons:

---

28 Deanna Ting, "Nine Months in, Apple News+ Isn't Wowing Publishers," *Digiday*, December 17, 2019, https://digiday.com/media/nine-months-apple-news-isnt-wowing-publishers/.

- There is a new event-based data model that allows for easier data aggregation across both web and app properties.
- Privacy and data governance features are built into the GA4 platform for more control of your user data.
- GA4 was built with Google's machine learning capabilities that surface automated alerts and insights, power audience creation, and improve reporting and analysis.
- Google Signals will continue to allow for better cross-device user-tracking of anonymous visitors.
- GA4 will further make conversion rate optimization easier for news and media organizations with a subscription model by leveraging predictive metrics and audiences.

GA4 has an entirely new data model built off of Firebase Analytics's event-based model, meaning you no longer have different types of hits (page views, screen views, events, transactions, etc.). Every hit that gets sent to GA4 is an event to which you can include additional custom data for more comprehensive reporting and analysis.

Because previous versions of GA, like Universal Analytics (UA), used a slightly different data model depending on the platform, combining website data with app data was partially possible, though not entirely.

While you could combine the data into a single UA property, websites and apps used slightly different dimensions and metrics, like page (web dimension) vs. screen name (app dimension) and page views (web metric) vs. screen views (app metric). Because of these differences, it was difficult to aggregate web and app platforms together for combined metrics within UA properties.

Many of the news and media organizations we work with have a number of different digital platforms that they operate, including mobile and OTT apps (not just websites). Now that GA4 finally uses the same data model across platforms, the aggregation of that data is much simpler and more powerful.

Another important benefit of GA4 for news and media organizations is the privacy and data governance features built into the platform. We've found many decision-makers take a privacy-first view to protect consumer data and preserve trust when adopting new digital platforms, so Google has ensured that GA4 was built with privacy and data governance in mind.

GA4 was also built with Google's vast machine learning models to be able to surface trends and insights automatically. Google is doubling-down on its machine learning abilities to power alerts, audiences, reports, metrics, and more. They will continue to build new machine learning capabilities into GA4, which will help organizations get insights quicker and easier and power more sophisticated marketing and advertising.

Google has also continued to build out its cookieless tracking solution that was first introduced in Universal Analytics. Called Google Signals, it allows Google to track users who have opted in to ads personalization across devices as long as they're signed in to a Google service on those devices. Most of us are signed in to at least one Google service on all the devices we own (e.g., Gmail, Google Photos, Google Drive/Google Docs, Google Workspace, and more). Because of this, Google is able to understand that one user is using multiple devices.

Universal Analytics leverages Signals to track users across your websites and apps, which allows Google to deduplicate your user data if those users are browsing anonymously and aren't signed in. There are only a few cross-device reports available right now in Universal Analytics, so it's very limited. However, our hope is that Google will continue to expand the use of Signals to power the user metric in more GA4 reporting instances as cookies continue to get limited by web browsers like Firefox and Safari.

Finally, GA4 will continue to make conversion rate optimization easier for news and media organizations with a subscription model by leveraging predictive metrics and audiences for targeting. There are a few predictive metrics available right now in Universal Analytics, like *conversion probability*, and GA4 will build on these to introduce new predictive capabilities powered by machine learning to improve conversion rates.

Hopefully, this list of GA4 benefits specific to news and media organizations gets you excited about the future of analytics measurements from Google. We're excited to help our clients take advantage of Google's next generation of Google Analytics.

HOW GA4 CAN DRIVE ANALYTICS MATURITY

Many of GA4's features are built with machine learning and automation in mind, which should help surface insights quicker, alert you sooner, and make your reporting and analysis more effective. These features will enable organizations to drive analytics value more quickly with fewer people and less budget.

Google is handling more of the processing and analysis with GA4 so, organizations with bandwidth constraints can still take advantage of advanced analytics capabilities normally reserved for much larger companies.

One of the biggest challenges that news and media organizations face when it comes to analytics maturity, as discussed earlier in the chapter, is the lack of first-party data. Large anonymous audiences aren't helpful for organizations in the business of connecting visitors with advertisers. GA4's predictive machine learning capabilities could potentially solve some of these issues, allowing publishers to create more granular, targeted audiences based on predictive behavior like "users most likely to convert" or "users with the highest predicted engagement" across platforms.

Also, because GA4 is user-centric and makes tracking users across platforms much easier, these audiences can now be more easily targeted based on the interactions across platforms. This was much more difficult to do in Universal Analytics.

Google Analytics 4 hasn't been fully built out yet, but Google will continue to innovate to bring more value to its end users. As more features get added, GA4 should allow organizations to do more with less, advancing their capabilities and, ultimately, their analytics maturity.

CHAPTER NINE

DIGITAL ANALYTICS MATURITY

CONSUMER PACKAGED GOODS

CHAPTER CONTRIBUTOR: CHRIS VAUGHAN

It's not unusual for global consumer packaged goods (CPG) and fast-moving consumer goods (FMCG) organizations to operate in almost every country in the world, requiring them to manage hundreds, if not thousands, of websites. The sheer size and complexity of these organizations lead to several unique challenges that make it difficult for them to advance their digital analytics maturity.

THE DANGERS OF DECENTRALIZED DATA

The struggles many global CPG and FMCG organizations have with digital analytics maturity start, quite literally, at the top. The fact is, high-ranking stakeholders within these massive organizations often lack a true appreciation of their digital assets (website, mobile apps, etc.) or the value those assets bring to the organization.

The reason for this is clear. Brick-and-mortar stores remain the primary distribution method for most CPG and FMCG products. Even with the rise of e-commerce shopping in the last twenty years, studies have shown that up to 90 percent of CPG products are still sold offline in places like Walmart, Kroger, and Target.

As a result, most global CPG organizations have little in the way of e-commerce offerings, and even less in terms of direct-to-consumer offerings, where products are sold through an owned website or app rather than a retailer like Amazon. Consequently, the vast majority of websites and apps owned by large CPG organizations are designed to do one of three things:

- Inform current and potential customers about a brand or product.
- Promote current and upcoming products or campaigns.
- Generate customer loyalty and engagement with the brand.

None of these things directly generate revenue, and therein lies the problem. Most CPG websites and apps don't sell products, so they aren't directly impacting the bottom line. This is why so many high-ranking executives overlook websites and apps or view them as something they must have simply because everyone else has them. Executives won't invest more than minimal resources to analyze their websites and apps, and the analytics maturity of the organization suffers, with many large CPG organizations stuck in the nascent stage.

For those organizations lucky enough to get executive buy-in, however, the massive size and breadth of these global organizations impose their own set of challenges to be overcome.

For starters, with a plethora of individual brands, each of which might be sold in dozens of countries around the world, most CPG organizations are forced to maintain a decentralized analytics strategy.

This means that analytics decisions are made separately by individual market or brand teams based on each team's unique needs. This can be a good thing if done correctly; after all, it makes sense for teams to collect data about the things that are important to them. In practice, though, it becomes difficult to standardize across the entire organization because individual markets or brands will have access to widely varying levels of people, processes, and platforms.

As a result, some markets or brands will have highly intricate and advanced analytics strategies, integrating data across multiple platforms and using a holistic view of the customer journey to drive optimizations to their audiences and digital media campaigns. However, others will be less advanced, deploying incredibly basic strategies that look purely at vanity metrics rather than those markers that could lead to real change for the organization.

Those less-advanced organizations will typically lack technical expertise (people), effective strategies for data collection and analysis (processes), and top-notch integrations between disparate data sources (platforms). These gaps signal that these less mature markets or brands will have inherently lower quality data from which to make business decisions about their websites, apps, and marketing campaigns. It also means they will lack a holistic view of their customers, and without that holistic view, they won't be able to optimize their marketing campaigns, resulting in wasteful spending that could total in the millions of dollars.

This fragmented strategy causes problems for a global team when they attempt to assess the collective performance of all their digital assets. When individual markets have widely varying analytics strategies, it becomes almost impossible for a central analytics team to collect "apples to apples" data from their entire portfolio of websites and apps. With hundreds or thousands of digital assets, this can cause a real problem for any CPG organization looking to assess which assets are driving tangible value to the organization and which are lagging behind.

The lack of standardization has caused even bigger problems for Global CPG organizations in recent years, as the rise of privacy regulations has made it more critical than ever for businesses to know exactly what data they're collecting about their users and how they're collecting that data. This is hard enough for companies with a single website or app. For global CPG organizations with hundreds or thousands of digital assets, it can be an absolute nightmare.

This puts global CPG organizations in a very precarious situation. As we discussed in our chapter on customer data governance, fines for violating laws like GDPR and CCPA are substantial, especially for multibillion-dollar organizations operating in countries around the world. In order to ensure compliance with these regulations, CPG organizations must be able to consistently monitor all of the data being collected by the websites and apps set up in markets around the world.

Without an enterprise-level monitoring tool, these organizations are left to hope that one of their individual markets or brands won't inadvertently track something on a website that will trigger a privacy fine. That's easier said than done, especially if an organization doesn't value the data they are collecting across their portfolio of digital assets.

As you can see, global CPG and FMCG organizations face a host of challenges that prevent them from advancing their digital analytics maturity. Many of them, as a result, remain nascent. However, in recent years, a few CPG companies have managed to start moving swiftly through the maturity stages as they've become more data-driven.

If you're a stakeholder in a CPG organization, how can you tell where your organization falls? As with other industries, it comes down to the 6 Ps of Digital Analytics Transformation: purpose, people, platforms, processes, pace, and payoff. As we examine the stages of maturity for a CPG organization, we will consider each of these and how they change as the company progresses.

STARTING WITH THE BASICS: NASCENT CPG

For Global CPG and FMCG organizations, as with most industries, the nascent stage is often marked by a lack of true *purpose* for digital analytics. These companies are at the baseline level of digital analytics strategy. They know they should be collecting customer data, and they've probably deployed the basic, out-of-the-box version of Google Analytics. However, the organization as a whole hasn't yet defined a why for the data they want to collect because they don't really understand how data can help their business.

As a result, they're not spending resources to take their analytics implementation to the next level. This also means that they're missing out on the higher-level functionalities that Google Analytics could provide to add value to the organization.

The lack of purpose has a direct impact on the *people* within the organization as well, but due to their sheer size, global CPG organizations in the nascent stage are structured a bit differently. Generally, analytics decision-making tends to lie with the global team with very little analytics expertise at the market or brand level.

Additionally, stakeholders in nascent CPG organizations tend to operate in silos, focusing only on the specific data or initiatives they believe are important without getting feedback from others in the organization. Key stakeholders in the customer journey, such as marketing and media teams, are rarely consulted about what data they want access to and which metrics or KPIs would fuel success.

In terms of platforms, CPG organizations in the nascent stage typically view the data from their enterprise analytics tool as the only source of truth. Google Analytics stakeholders might not know that other tools within the organization are also collecting data about how customers engage with their digital assets, or they probably don't believe that these other tools are even relevant to them. As a result, there are no integrations between the enterprise analytics *platform* and other disparate data sources, which prevents the organization from having a 360-degree view of the customer journey for their brands.

The *processes* in nascent CPG organizations are usually quite basic. Since the organization is probably only utilizing the out-of-the-box version of Google Analytics, its global analytics team only has access to basic metrics that may not be actionable. As a result, their team may be focused on data that their market or brand stakeholders can't use for any meaningful purpose.

For example, the basic version of Google Analytics has a metric called bounce rate, which reveals the number of times a user navigated to a page on the website and then left without viewing other pages or completing any activities, such as clicking on a link. The tricky thing about bounce rate, though, is that it doesn't tell you why the user left the page. Maybe they didn't like the content, or maybe they found exactly the content they needed to solve their problem. There's no way to tell.

However, a nascent CPG organization might use that baseline metric to determine which of their digital assets is best at keeping users engaged. They'll reach out to brand website managers with high bounce rates and tell them their website is underperforming. The brand managers, in turn, have no idea how to improve their website performance because the basic metrics don't provide any additional context for the high bounce rate. These managers begin to distrust the data, and the chances of the organization becoming truly data-driven are remote.

Due to the centralized digital analytics strategy and decision-making of their core team, you might expect that a global CPG organization can move at a quick pace. However, we find that these teams tend to get set in their ways, doing the same things in the same ways as they've always done them, which tends to make the pace of progress incredibly slow. Since nascent teams rarely communicate with stakeholders in other parts of the organization, they also tend to sit in "thought vacuums" where they only consider their own insights into improving the organization's digital analytics strategy.

The sheer size of these organizations also affects the *pace* of their change. In the rare instance, when a CPG organization's global team decides to enact a change to their digital analytics strategy, the change has to be carried out on hundreds of websites around the world. With few, if any, experts at the market or brand level who can roll out these changes, the organization encounters an extreme bottleneck as they attempt to update all of their assets. This bottleneck makes the process long and arduous, which ensures that changes are few and far between.

Given these unique challenges, it's no wonder that the digital analytics *payoff* for nascent CPG organizations tends to be low. Data and analysis of digital assets are rarely seen by anyone outside of the central team. Even when data is circulated, it lacks context, which makes it unactionable. As a result, other users within the organization become distrustful of the data, and organizational stakeholders make "gut feeling" decisions instead of data-driven decisions.

If this whole scenario seems a bit extreme, bear in mind, we've seen it over and over again in our work with global CPG and multi-brand organizations. Fortunately, escaping the nascent stage is entirely possible, as long as you focus on the 6 Ps.

EMERGING GIANTS

A CPG or FMCG organization begins to enter the emerging stage when its purpose changes and they begin focusing on the real business questions that their data can help the organization answer rather than just collecting data for the sake of collecting it. This shift in mindset is huge, particularly when it comes to the people involved in the overall digital analytics strategy.

No longer can the global analytics team think only about themselves and their own needs. In the emerging stage, they begin to consider the thoughts, opinions, and needs of other teams and functions within the organization.

First, the global team begins to develop a relationship with higher-level executives in the organization, perhaps even C-suite members like the CIO, CMO, or CDO (Chief Data Officer). In a nascent organization, these executives are often disengaged from websites and apps, placing little value on them or the data that they collect. However, in an emerging organization, they begin to see the value in their digital asset portfolio, so they become interested in the value these digital assets can provide to the business. The digital analytics team needs to work closely with these stakeholders to discover what their needs are and how the data being collected can provide insights to help guide their key business decisions.

Next, the analytics team needs to develop close relationships with various marketing and media teams within the organization, maintaining regular communication with those teams to discuss any upcoming campaigns and related objectives. Armed with this information, the analytics team can make sure they track the right in-app or on-site elements to provide valuable insights about key metrics that can make marketing campaigns successful.

This relationship between analytics and marketing is absolutely critical for digital analytics maturity. With the right strategy, tracking, and analysis, digital analytics can directly affect the ROI of an organization's digital marketing campaigns by providing valuable insights into which campaigns are most effective at getting users to convert. This can lead to significant optimization in an organization's digital marketing, allowing them to increase spending on effective campaigns while reallocating spending from the ineffective ones.

Finally, and perhaps most importantly, global analytics teams in emerging CPG organizations begin working closely with users in individual markets, brands, and business units. We call these users "Local Analytics Champions" (LACs), and they are of paramount importance for large global CPG companies that want to increase their digital analytics maturity.

With hundreds of brands operating in dozens of countries, it's simply not possible for global analytics teams in massive CPG organizations to understand the analytics needs of each market or brand around the world. This makes Local Analytics Champions incredibly beneficial, as they become extensions of the global team, providing eyes and ears on the ground in each market and for each brand. They can, in turn, provide additional insights about the unique needs of their markets and brands to the global team. On a local level, LACs advocate the company's digital analytics strategy to business units, reducing implementation time for new analytics initiatives and processes.

While all of these developments are great, there remains one big problem with Local Analytics Champions in emerging organizations. Chiefly, these local users tend to have widely varying technical skillsets and knowledge, which typically depend on the market's individual budget. For instance, an "LAC" in a smaller market may have a very limited analytics background and may not be able to provide much help in identifying local analytics opportunities or use cases.

On the other hand, LACs in markets with larger budgets tend

to have a more robust analytics background and are able to help deploy new tracking or configure new analytics instances to reduce the heavy lifting for both global analytics and local development teams.

Even if their contributions are inconsistent from market to market, the rise of Local Analytics Champions is a vital step in the right direction for a CPG organization heading into the emerging stage.

In terms of platforms, emerging CPG organizations begin taking advantage of advanced analytics features and functionalities to drive additional value from their data collection, reporting, and insights. An organization using Google Analytics will typically move from the free version to the enterprise edition at this point.

At the same time, emerging CPG organizations rely less on out-of-the-box metrics and start creating their own custom solutions to track specific user activities on their websites and mobile apps. Identifying these user activities (called "event tracking" in Google Analytics) requires a more strategic digital analytics mindset, and the implementation of such tracking often requires significant development work in the website and app source code. The payoff for such investments, however, can be huge since advanced tracking enables an organization to gain valuable insights about how users interact with their digital assets, in turn, providing clear answers to key business questions.

At the emerging level, these changes aren't yet holistic throughout the entire organization due to variations in markets and brands, as well as differences in the knowledge and expertise of individual LACs. Some business units will start utilizing more advanced event tracking, and others won't. This lack of standardization is par for the course in an emerging CPG organization.

In the emerging stage, CPG analytics stakeholders also begin getting more exposure to the organization's other data collection platforms as cross-functional team relationships start to develop. Each of these platforms has the opportunity to help the organization gain additional insight into their customer's journey; however, emerging organizations rarely integrate all of these platforms in a way that provides a full 360-degree view of the customer. There are a couple of reasons for this.

First, they may not be utilizing platforms that can be easily connected to extend available data, particularly if they're using platforms that are developed by different software companies. Maybe they use Google Analytics, but instead of Display & Video 360, they use a programmatic media platform designed by another software company. In that case, they are missing out on the benefits of seamless integration between Google's products, which means they lack valuable insights about the performance of their media campaigns. This contributes to a fragmented view of the customer journey.

Second, even when organizations rely on platforms that easily integrate, they may still miss out on some insights because of the varying levels of technical expertise among their Local Analytics Champions. Just because platforms can integrate doesn't mean LACs have sufficient knowledge to take advantage of the integrations that will create value for the organization. As a result, it's left to the global team to pick up the slack in order to take full advantage of platform integration that will create that holistic view of the customer journey. Given the pure size of the organization, this is often easier said than done.

In terms of process, emerging CPG organizations are beginning to operate more efficiently, and Local Analytics Champions are making it easier to roll out new initiatives in a timely manner. At a local level, the LACs are able to optimize their own analytics implementations based on the needs of their business units. However, glaring holes remain in the standardization of data.

At least some local market and brand teams at this stage have the ability to make data-driven decisions, thanks to their advanced analytics strategies and cross-platform integrations. They are now continuously improving the performance of their digital assets and marketing campaigns, driving more money and better results to the overall organization.

Less mature market and brand teams, however, are still relying on out-of-the-box metrics. As a result, they are not yet data-driven, using gut feelings rather than real insights about digital assets and marketing campaigns. This situation can cause the global team to favor data from more mature markets and brands when making strategic decisions about the global analytics strategy.

Fortunately, pace is where emerging CPG organizations begin to shine. Thanks to Local Analytics Champions, global analytics teams can quickly circulate insights and strategic information throughout the organization. Markets and brands with technical expertise can implement advanced tracking of user activities, driving more powerful business decisions. Additionally, regular communication now takes place among the analytics, marketing, and executive teams, allowing for ongoing optimization of analytics and marketing strategies. At last, organizations are beginning to realize the true value of their digital analytics strategy.

All is not perfect, however, as the quickening pace is inconsistent due to the varying levels of maturity and expertise across markets and brands. Some business units react and adapt quickly to needed changes, while others simply can't. Additionally, the insights gained from cross-team communication can seem like a firehose of information to some local teams, requiring a significant amount of time and effort to sort out the prioritization of organizational initiatives.

Even with these challenges, however, the pace is accelerating, and the organization is beginning to see the payoff. The chief payoff for an emerging CPG organization is that the organization as a whole has begun to take digital analytics seriously. While every team is not yet data-driven, more and more business decisions are based on digital analytics insights.

Key organizational stakeholders are beginning to trust the data, giving team members opportunities to showcase their expertise to executives, which fosters career growth for analytics-minded individuals. As those individuals rise in the ranks, an even stronger analytics mindset is instilled in the company.

There remains a lot of work to be done, but the emerging company is already pulling ahead of many of its global CPG counterparts.

GETTING CONNECTED

In the connected stage, everything starts to come together for the company from a digital analytics standpoint. Reaching this stage is a real achievement for a large, global CPG organization since they have hundreds of digital assets in their portfolio and a similar number of stakeholders relying on data for decision-making.

As with other stages of the digital analytics maturity framework, reaching the connected stage starts with an organization's purpose for digital analytics. For global CPG organizations, this purpose is to use their first-party digital data to build a comprehensive, 360-degree view of their ideal customer's journey across all of their digital assets. Being able to achieve such a lofty goal requires significant "leveling up" of all 6 P's, starting with the people who are deploying and using the digital analytics data.

In the emerging stage, Local Analytics Champions within each business unit act as extensions of the global analytics team to relay the needs of individual markets and brands. However, the maturity of these LACs varies widely, creating significant fragmentation and making it difficult to standardize data or implement analytics practices from one brand to the next.

At the connected stage, however, Local Analytics Champions all have similar levels of analytics knowledge and expertise. As a result, the entire digital analytics function within the organization operates as one big, well-oiled machine. Global analytics initiatives are no longer developed in a vacuum by the global team because they now regularly communicate with LACs to identify their specific digital objectives and KPIs.

This higher level of engagement, as well as the consistent technical level of LACs, enables initiatives to be implemented quickly and correctly within each market or brand. As a result, the global team has the apples-to-apples data they need to make collective assessments of the overall digital asset portfolio within the organization.

In the spirit of continuous improvement, Local Analytics Champions share ongoing feedback about the effectiveness of global strategies, as well as the unique implementations happening in their local market that could be adapted to others. No stakeholders are left behind, as the entire analytics function in the organization becomes more data-driven, collecting better data to make better business decisions.

Relationships between marketing and executive teams continue to strengthen as well, with more frequent communication and sharing of knowledge. All teams now know exactly which metrics and KPIs the other teams need to be successful, and nonanalytics users trust the digital data enough to rely on it for business decisions.

The most important person at this stage, however, is the customer. The organization's focus on using digital analytics to gain a comprehensive picture of the customer improves the end user's experience. First-party analytics data allows them to build more targeted remarketing lists, so the organization is able to show more relevant ads. In so doing, they avoid bothering users with non-personalized marketing messages.

Additionally, a greater level of customer knowledge creates more opportunities for personalized content, ensuring that any potential customer who uses one of the organization's websites or mobile apps gets an experience tailored to the specific stage of their unique customer journey.

Finally, collecting better and more holistic data about customers also enables organizations to provide better, more relevant products based on the wants and needs of their customer base. In recent years, more CPG organizations have begun utilizing their digital assets to collect qualitative feedback from customers about what they would like to see in future product developments. This is a great way for connected CPG analytics teams to continue driving value despite a lack of revenue-generating functionalities on their websites and mobile apps.

Gaining a holistic view of the customer goes beyond the people, though. The organization also needs to start using specialized platforms that are built for the exact tasks they want to perform or data they want to connect. As much as possible, these platforms should be natively integrated with one another to provide additional insights and value to the organization.

An enterprise-level analytics platform, such as Analytics 360, must be present in CPG organizations in the connected stage for the company to take full advantage of advanced data collection and analysis functionalities. Connected organizations track user behavior and activities at a granular level on their digital assets, giving them the ability to monitor key functionalities and content that drive users to convert with a desired action.

Beyond that, most global CPG organizations at this stage utilize a plethora of software, such as customer relationship management (CRM) tools, programmatic digital media platforms, search bidding and management tools, and a data warehouse. Each of these tools has a specific purpose, and being able to natively integrate them enables an organization to extend its overall view of a customer's engagement online. These integrations also ensure an organization makes business-case decisions based on first-party data generated by interconnected platforms, which is more important than ever in today's privacy-focused world where third-party data is becoming less impactful.

On the topic of privacy regulations, CPG organizations in the connected stage must take special care to monitor and govern all data being collected across their many websites and mobile apps. This task can be difficult for organizations of any size, but for large organizations with hundreds of digital assets and millions of hits being collected every month, complying with regulations like GDPR and CCPA across all markets and brands becomes incredibly complicated.

Fortunately, tools exist to make this easier. Tag Inspector can be a CPG organization's best compliance friend as it monitors tags and the associated cookies dropped on each site. InfoTrust's proprietary Analytics Monitoring Solution (infotrust.com/ams) detects irregularities and discrepancies, as well as the collection of personally identifiable information. Using these kinds of tools can help give large CPG organizations peace of mind and protect them against hefty government fines that come from potential privacy violations.

Connected-stage CPG organizations are also improving their analytics processes by taking advantage of efficiencies to streamline the collection and activation of their data. The organization has standardized the collection of key data points, naming conventions, and configurations, ensuring that all organizational KPIs can be quickly and easily referenced for business decision-making. As a result, stakeholders are able to determine which websites, apps, and marketing campaigns are driving the most value, so they can replicate those successes across other digital assets.

Having interconnected and integrated platforms also make it easier to gain better data about customers, giving marketing and executive teams regular insights about the holistic customer journey across all of their digital assets. This data allows them to make more powerful optimizations to their digital presence, increasing the ROI of digital marketing activities. Furthermore, this establishes a cycle of continuous improvements, with analytics data informing marketing optimizations, which then power more accurate data collection.

The pace of a connected-stage CPG organization is quick and efficient. Regular discussions take place between analytics, marketing, and executive teams, ensuring that everyone is on the same page about which data to collect and how best to deliver it for maximum impact. Plus, since Local Analytics Champions all have similar skill levels now, global strategies can be implemented quickly across all markets and brands.

Additionally, the use of enterprise-level data governance and monitoring tools means that any missteps in user privacy collection can be remedied fast, protecting the organization from accidental violations that could cost them millions.

Clearly, the payoff of these advancements can be huge. When a CPG organization can get a clear, 360-degree view of its customer's journey across all of its digital assets, that data supercharges its online marketing and user engagement. This leads to massive ROI, ensuring that the organization is investing in marketing campaigns and technology that add tangible value to the organization while also making it easy to identify and cut wasteful marketing spending.

Still, the journey doesn't stop there. There is one more level of digital analytics maturity that a global CPG organization should strive for.

MULTI-MOMENT CPG SUCCESS

Multi-moment CPG organizations build on the foundation of effective people, platforms, and processes established at the connected stage. They've worked hard to gain a holistic, 360-degree view of the customer journey, which establishes their new purpose of using that data to predict future successes with marketing campaigns, products, and digital assets. This means introducing a new element to their digital analytics strategy, data science.

The people who will help make this happen will either be a team of data scientists within the organization or a third-party provider who specializes in developing advanced insights. Typically, these data scientists work closely with analytics users at the global level, but some organizations also employ them for more advanced local market and brand teams as well.

The process for these data scientists is simple: take the huge amount of data coming in from all the digital assets throughout the world and use that data to predict future successes based on past results. To do this effectively, the data science team may use a number of different forecasting techniques, including customer lifetime value forecasting, propensity modeling, audience scoring, and sales forecasting, with the last technique being especially important for CPG organizations with significant direct-to-consumer functionalities.

We talked about some of these forecasting models in the chapter on Google Cloud for Marketing, but for a CPG organization, each of these techniques has unique and specific use cases. For example, audience scoring techniques look at past user behavior on a website in order to predict which users are most likely to perform specific actions that the organization, market, or brand wants them to perform. Using sophisticated modeling, data scientists then output a unique score for each user based on past behavior and their future likelihood to convert. These scores can then be imported into an analytics platform or data warehouse, giving the organization opportunities to create targeted marketing campaigns tailored to those users who are most likely to convert.

CPG data scientists rely heavily on having solid platforms for analytics and marketing, with strong integrations in place throughout the organization. They also regularly utilize data warehouse tools such as BigQuery, as well as wider suites of predictive modeling and machine learning tools like those available in Google Cloud Platform. These powerful tools, combined with strong and comprehensive data collection, empower data scientists to uncover highly insightful analysis that can effectively predict the future success of marketing campaigns and on-site promotions.

The payoff at this stage is huge. The ability to predict the lifetime value of customers and determine the future success of marketing campaigns means that the organization has effectively "hacked" the sales funnel. As a result, they can proactively improve their marketing campaigns to maximize their value and drive revenue back to the bottom line. In an industry where 90 percent of sales are conducted offline, this creates incredible opportunities for the organization to continuously add value with their digital assets throughout the world.

A CASE STUDY IN CPG SPLIT MATURITY

Given the massive size and scope of most Global CPG and FMCG organizations, it's possible for a CPG company to be at any of these maturity stages globally but have individual markets or brands at higher or lower stages. For an example of how this works, let's consider the case of one of InfoTrust's global CPG partners.

Partner A (as we'll call them) is one of the largest CPG organizations in the world, with more than a thousand digital assets across hundreds of brands in dozens of countries. When we started working with them, they were in a low emerging stage of digital analytics maturity. Today, they've reached the connected stage, with a primary purpose of assembling that holistic view of their online customer to power business and marketing decisions from their first-party digital data.

Globally, they have a solid assemblage of people, platforms, and processes. They've deployed Local Analytics Champions into each significant market around the world, and leaders regularly engage these LACs in two-way conversations so they can pass along new strategic directions and learn about the analytics tactics working in individual markets. Additionally, analytics teams work closely with both global and local marketing teams so all marketing needs are understood and taken into consideration when any changes are discussed for the overall digital analytics strategy.

Partner A utilizes the entire Google Marketing Platform suite for digital analytics (Google Analytics, Google Tag Manager), digital media (Campaign Manager, Display & Video 360, Search Ads 360), and site optimization (Optimize). Where relevant, these platforms are integrated with each other to ensure that they provide the organization with comprehensive information about the performance of digital assets and marketing campaigns.

Additionally, Partner A combines Google Marketing Platform data in BigQuery along with data from other tools, such as their global CRM tool. This allows data scientists to utilize powerful modeling techniques to create a clear view of their customers as they utilize the company's digital assets. The organization can then use that information to create more effective marketing campaigns and website optimizations, improving the customer experience and creating more loyal users.

Because of their large, multinational online presence, Partner A also has a strong focus on customer data governance. Using both Tag Inspector and InfoTrust's Analytics Monitoring Tool, they ensure all data being collected from their digital assets has clear user consent and is collected according to local and regional privacy regulations. When a violation is discovered, they move quickly and efficiently to resolve the problem, whether that means adjusting an erroneous tag deployed by a third-party agency or modifying site code to eliminate the collection of personally identifiable information (PII).

Their processes are also solid. Together with InfoTrust, Partner A has put an impressive digital analytics strategy in place that includes standardized configurations of analytics platforms, tracking for key user activities on their websites, and common naming conventions for all of their global analytics elements. They also make strong use of the data layer on their websites, allowing them to collect incredibly granular information about their websites, pages, and users.

With this information, organizational stakeholders can get greater insights from reporting while also developing more powerful remarketing audiences. Plus, since all of their relevant analytics and marketing platforms are integrated, the insights provided by these tools contribute beautifully to the efforts of both the analytics and marketing teams. They have built a true cycle of improvement: analytics data helps optimize marketing campaigns, and marketing campaigns provide better, more holistic analytics data.

Though Partner A has put the right people, platforms, and processes in place to become a truly connected organization, they still have a few business units that are far less mature than the global company is. These markets tend to have higher turnover in their Local Analytics Champions, so they often lack the technical expertise and knowledge of Partner A's detailed standards. As a result, those markets aren't able to utilize digital analytics as effectively as other markets or brands.

This high LAC turnover also prevents the establishment of strong relationships with other analytics and marketing teams around the world, and so the continuous cycle of improvement in these markets isn't as effective. While the organization is connected, these challenges cause the lagging markets or brands to still operate in the emerging stage.

At the same time, a few of their markets and brands have truly reached the multi-moment stage of the maturity framework, surpassing the global organization. These business units have highly advanced digital analytics strategies in place, with incredibly intricate tracking and strong integrations among all relevant platforms. As a result, they can push their data into the BigQuery data warehouse and use advanced data science techniques to not only see the holistic customer journey but predictively model the success of upcoming marketing campaigns and product promotions.

These business units set an example for the rest of the organization, not only by showing other markets and brands what is possible with a strong digital analytics strategy but also by using data to optimize both their products and digital marketing, thus driving more revenue to the bottom-line of the organization.

THE VALUE OF GOOGLE ANALYTICS 4 FOR CPG

As with most industries, the new Google Analytics 4 (GA4) properties will have a tremendous impact on the way that Global CPG, FMCG, and multi-brand organizations collect and analyze digital data. As you might expect, the sheer size and decentralized nature of these organizations will also present unique challenges when they begin to migrate from the current iteration of Google Analytics (called "Universal Analytics," or UA) to GA4.

In this section, we'll look at some of the key impacts that GA4 properties will have on Global CPG organizations and discuss how analytics professionals in these companies can mitigate some of the challenges that they'll encounter with migration to GA4.

MAPPING A PATH TO SUCCESS

Let's start by addressing the biggest impact: the overall data collection model of GA4 properties is *very* different from UA properties. While we won't deep-dive into that new data collection model in this chapter (check out the Google Analytics 4 chapter earlier in the book for more details), the key thing to remember is that the GA4 data collection model is event-based, meaning any activity that occurs on a website (and is tracked in a GA4 property) is treated as an event. This is a significant change from the UA data collection model, which is based primarily around page views and sessions and treats event-tracking as an additional form of tracking not included "out of the box."

For businesses in all industries, this changing data collection model will necessitate a significant data migration exercise. Existing Google Analytics events, which use a category/action/label hierarchy to present information about the event that occurred on the site, will need to be mapped to the new GA4 structure, which doesn't use the category/action/label hierarchy. Any existing custom dimensions or metrics that are being collected in Universal Analytics properties will need to be mapped over to corresponding GA4 custom parameters or user properties, and goals that are currently being used in UA will need to be reestablished in GA4 as "conversions."

Ironically, CPG and multi-brand organizations in the earlier stages of analytics maturity will have an easier time completing these activities than their more mature counterparts. For instance, companies in the nascent stage will probably need to worry only about mapping their existing global GA standards, if any, to GA4, since market or brand strategies will likely be either nonexistent or controlled wholly by local teams.

On the other hand, more mature CPG organizations in the emerging or connected stages will also need to develop comprehensive GA4 guidance and education plans for their Local Analytics Champions to ensure that their LACs are able to facilitate the mapping of individual market or brand UA standards over to GA4.

For large organizations like those in the CPG industry, mapping an existing digital analytics strategy over to the new GA4 properties will be a time-consuming task, but the real "heavy lifting" for analytics professionals begins when the mapping exercise has been completed. That's because in order for brands to begin taking advantage of the new GA4 properties, any existing Universal Analytics tracking code and tags that are in place today will need to be modified or completely redeployed.

For organizations using Google's Global Site Tag (gTag), they will need to modify each tracking code snippet to ensure that the tag begins sending data to the GA4 property. Companies using a tag management system like Google Tag Manager will need to ensure that each of their tag manager assets across the entire organization is updated with GA4 code snippets and tag templates.

As you might imagine, redeploying all of these tag assets can be a struggle even for organizations with only a single website. However, for Global CPG organizations, updating every Google Analytics tag that's firing across dozens, hundreds, or thousands of websites can seem daunting.

REPORTING TO THE RESCUE

Luckily, GA4 properties are much more than simply an updated data collection model. The core reporting functionalities of GA4 have been completely overhauled as well. While Universal Analytics properties have over 150 out-of-the-box reports that provide insights about website usage patterns, the new GA4 properties have less than twenty (at the time of this writing).

Accounting for this gap, GA4 properties have much stronger ad hoc reporting features than their UA counterparts. The new "Analysis Hub" in GA4, for instance, gives analytics stakeholders the ability to create more powerful customized reports than have ever been available in Universal Analytics properties.

GA4 properties also come with the promise of increased machine learning and predictive analysis tools, which go far beyond what is available in Universal Analytics. As a result, GA4 gives reporting stakeholders the ability to create predictive audiences or determine an estimated lifetime value for a customer based on their website activity, reducing the reporting overhead required to get these key insights about a customer's journey through a brand website.

These new reporting advancements will be incredibly beneficial for CPG/FMCG organizations, which typically have large numbers of reporting stakeholders with varying levels of analytics maturity. For example, machine learning and predictive analytics will help less technical stakeholders get advanced insights quickly, without having to worry about creating their own complex reports. On the other hand, more advanced stakeholders will be able to take full advantage of the Analysis Hub to fully customize their digital analytics reporting in a way that showcases the unique business objectives and KPIs of their brand/market assets to organizational stakeholders.

Despite these positives, however, the new reporting in GA4 will also pose some significant challenges for CPG organizations. For starters, any business that has been invested in Universal Analytics for an extended period of time is probably relying on some of the traditional UA reports (either out-of-the-box or custom reports) to showcase website metrics to their stakeholders. With the new data-collection model in GA4 properties, GA4 reports will look very different than the UA reporting that organizational stakeholders are used to seeing.

Common metrics that are prevalent in many current UA reports, such as the number of page views or sessions, will look quite different in GA4 reports where everything is treated as an event (even page views and sessions). Additionally, some reporting options that might be used to influence key business decisions today simply don't exist anymore in GA4, such as the event category/action/label hierarchy.

As a result of these shifts, businesses will be forced to reimagine and recreate their current Universal Analytics reports as new GA4 versions. Unfortunately, this is an area where analytics professionals in Global CPG/FMCG organizations will feel the pain. Part of this "pain" will be due to the sheer volume of assets and reports that will need to be updated in order to transition the entire organization, including all brands and markets around the world, to the new GA4 reporting formats.

Beyond that, analytics teams and Local Analytics Champions should also be prepared to personally train their reporting stakeholders about the new GA4 reports and the valuable insights that those reports can provide. This training and education will be time-consuming, but it's absolutely necessary to ensure the future-state adoption and activation of GA4 data throughout the organization.

Make no mistake, the work that will be required for CPG organizations to fully transition to Google Analytics 4 will be significant, but it will be well worth it. In our view, the new event-based data collection model and reporting options of GA4 properties make it much easier for organizational stakeholders to understand how their customers use brand websites to move toward a desired conversion. As with any change, though, there's a "change curve" that the organization will inevitably have to go through to reach the new reality.

So, how can analytics professionals in CPG organizations help accelerate their teams through the GA4 change curve? From our experience working with dozens of global CPG/FMCG brands, we offer three main tips to help:

1. Plan now to ensure future success.
2. Dual-tag, but keep your single source of truth (for now).
3. Don't wait to educate.

PLAN NOW TO ENSURE FUTURE SUCCESS

As mentioned earlier, because the new data-collection model of GA4 properties is so different from Universal Analytics properties, it will require all organizations to go through a significant data-mapping exercise in order to take advantage of the new GA4 features and benefits. Additionally, reporting, which is typically generated from Universal Analytics properties, will need to be completely overhauled in GA4 so that reporting stakeholders can continue getting the data they need to make key business decisions.

All of these changes would have a big impact on organizations with just a single website asset. For organizations with dozens, hundreds, or thousands (like many in the CPG industry), it can be a monumental undertaking.

As a result, we recommend that analytics professionals in CPG organizations start planning for their transition to GA4 as soon as possible. These users should begin working to map existing events, custom dimensions, custom metrics, and goals to their corresponding GA4 counterparts. They should start recreating GA4 versions of high-impact Universal Analytics reports, which are used to make key business decisions. Also, they should start circulating these new GA4 report versions to organizational stakeholders alongside the existing UA reports, so that these stakeholders can start getting comfortable with the GA4 data.

They should start doing this as soon as possible, but they should also be prepared to update these plans. The fact is, GA4 properties are still (as of this writing) in a "beta" status, so they will continue to be tweaked and optimized by Google over time. As a result, analytics professionals will likely need to revisit their GA4 migration strategies many times in the coming months to ensure that their plans account for any new GA4 features or functionalities that are released by Google.

DUAL-TAG BUT KEEP YOUR SINGLE SOURCE OF TRUTH (FOR NOW)

Along those same lines, because the GA4 properties are still in "beta" status, many organizations are afraid to use them today. However, it's important to note that the data-collection model of GA4 properties has been finalized, and we don't expect any major changes in the near future to the way data is collected and processed in GA4 properties.

It's imperative that organizations begin getting familiar with GA4 as the future of Google Analytics. The easiest way to do this is to begin dual-tagging as many digital assets as possible by deploying tags for GA4 properties alongside (not as a replacement to) the standard Universal Analytics tags that already exist on the website.

At the most basic level, getting this dual-tagging in place as soon as possible will help to build a lot of historical data in the new GA4 properties. This data can be incredibly beneficial in the future, as it will allow analytics stakeholders to provide extended reporting periods (quarter-on-quarter or year-on-year, for instance) once the organization completely migrates to GA4.

More importantly, dual-tagging your digital assets for GA4 will allow analytics teams and reporting stakeholders to begin seeing what the new GA4 properties are capable of. This will allow them to get familiar with GA4 data prior to a full transition in the future, which can be especially important for less technical stakeholders, who may need extended time to understand the differences between GA4 and UA.

On that note, analytics professionals in CPG organizations should keep Universal Analytics data as their "single source of truth" for the time being. While GA4 properties will undoubtedly bring tremendous value to CPG and FMCG organizations, teams should plan for an extended GA4 transition time to ensure that all stakeholders are comfortable making business decisions from the new GA4 data. In the end, UA properties aren't going away anytime soon, so there's no need to rush to completely replace the UA reporting and data that organizational stakeholders are so familiar with.

DON'T WAIT TO EDUCATE

Throughout this book, we've discussed numerous ways that GA4 properties differ from (and in many cases improve upon) Universal Analytics properties. These changes will have significant impacts on any organization that utilizes Google Analytics. However, they will be especially impactful on Global CPG organizations due to their sheer number of analytics stakeholders that are commonly scattered on market/brand teams throughout the world.

For most CPG/FMCG organizations, this plethora of stakeholders will have widely varying levels of Google Analytics knowledge and expertise. As a result, it is critical for these users to begin getting trained and educated on GA4 properties well in advance of transitioning to GA4 properties as the "single source of truth." Combined with the data that the organization will begin collecting through the dual-tagging of pilot GA4 properties, this training will give reporting stakeholders real-world use cases for GA4 reporting and showcase the tremendous features and benefits that GA4 properties have.

CHAPTER TEN

DIGITAL ANALYTICS MATURITY

RETAILERS AND E-COMMERCE/ DIRECT-TO-CONSUMER BRANDS

CHAPTER CONTRIBUTOR: AMIN SHAWKI, MICHELLE PLISKIN

 Michelle Pliskin is an Industry Team Lead for Info-Trust's e-commerce and retail clients, where she advises on executive strategic analytics initiatives through technical implementation. Having worked in both consulting and in-house capacities, she enjoys leveraging the breadth and depth of her analytics experience to help clients reach their business goals.

A NOTE BEFORE WE BEGIN

We finished the first edition of this book in July 2020, when people in many cities were being encouraged to stay home, except for essential needs, due to the COVID-19 pandemic. By the time you read this book, there's a good chance the world of retail has become very different. Gap, Lululemon, and many others have announced they are closing, and once COVID-19 is behind us, the retail landscape is likely to change forever, with even *more* emphasis on direct-to-consumer and e-commerce.

While there remains a lot of uncertainty and changes likely coming to the retail industry due to government lockdowns, we are confident that many of the principles we share will still hold true, especially as consumers resume their daily lives and normal buying habits. While not all retailers will survive the COVID-19 pandemic, the industry will inevitably move on, and the same fundamental principles will still apply.

At the end of 2019, shortly before contributing to this book, I had the privilege of becoming a new parent. My son, Charlie, is an amazing little nugget, but adjusting to this new parenting lifestyle has been, honestly, incredibly tiring. Don't get me wrong; I wouldn't trade this incredible time and my amazing boy for anything in the world, but any parent would be lying if they didn't admit it's hard. *Sleepless nights* is not an exaggeration. During my paternity leave (InfoTrust, a "Best Place to Work," gives us three months!), I had one particularly difficult day taking care of my son (I promise this relates to the topic at hand, so bear with me).

On this particular day, when Charlie was about six or seven weeks old, he did *not* want to take a nap. My wife and I hadn't left the house in a week, a feat made possible by Grubhub and Amazon, but that day, we decided it was time to take Charlie to the shopping mall for the first time for a little stroller nap time. While online shopping had made it possible to stay at home, we were getting cabin fever. Plus, we thought it might be interesting to see what the mall had to offer—a nice contrast to Amazon-style shopping. This was, of course, well before COVID-19 quarantines.

When we arrived at the mall, it was a relatively slow Tuesday afternoon. We put Charlie in the stroller and started walking around, and the whole place seemed especially quiet. There were dozens of stores, but only a few of them were busy. The Apple Store had a lot of customers, but they were mostly talking to customer service reps about their existing products and services. Almost all of the clothing retailers were empty. For the first time, I wondered if we were seeing the late stages of a dying mall.

Of course, we've all heard stories about the closing of brick-and-mortar stores, and we've read about the phenomenon of dead malls. Still, seeing how much the local shopping mall had changed shocked me. For decades, it had been a community meeting place, and now it was practically a ghost town. As we strolled around, we noticed mile markers on the walls and a walking path drawn on the floor. The mall had transformed from a busy retail outlet into an exercise course and product showcase. Even my wife and I spent our time just walking and window shopping. We didn't actually buy anything.

The retail world has been changing for years, and companies have become more reliant on their digital assets, but I'd never seen it so starkly. Indeed, as the InfoTrust team was finishing the first draft of this book, we read that Macy's had announced the closing of their Cincinnati headquarters and a move to New York City. Bose also announced the closing of all brick-and-mortar stores, as they move 100 percent online.

Retailers who embrace this change, moving more to e-commerce and a direct-to-consumer focus, putting digital analytics at the core of their operations, are poised to survive and thrive in this increasingly online retail world. Customers expect different but consistent interactions across all touchpoints, and the retailers who understand this are more likely to progress to multi-moment maturity.

But where should a retailer start? Let's take a look at the maturity framework and the 6 Ps for a retail organization.

BASIC-YET-CRITICAL NEEDS: NASCENT RETAILERS

As magical as it is to see Charlie happy and smiling, those sleepless nights of endless crying make parenting a real challenge. Like any baby, Charlie has basic needs that must be met, but we struggle as new parents to understand them sometimes. Why is he crying? Is he hungry? Tired? Does he need a diaper change? Is he going through a growth spurt? Is it gas? Is he just cranky?

Sometimes, it feels overwhelming, but we're learning to start with the key needs and iterate from there until he's happy again. If he's hungry, we feed him. That's the first and most important step. If that doesn't work, we try meeting his other needs until we discover the problem and resolve it.

Believe it or not, there's a lot of similarity between this story and the challenges of a retailer in the nascent maturity stage. Both parents of newborns and retailers are attempting to solve basic yet critical needs.

In the nascent stage, retailers have some basic digital analytics implemented within the organization, but the quality of the data is questionable, incomplete, or not solving key business challenges. Although data could solve critical needs within the organization, the basic KPIs are not being measured yet, or the organization isn't using the data for meaningful decision-making. Teams probably have a limited view of what actually drives performance or the ways data could be leveraged for decision-making to drive the business and marketing forward.

If you're in this stage right now, don't be discouraged. Nascent retailers aren't necessarily unsuccessful, and they have tremendous potential for growth. A focus on key conversion points will help you begin to make progress toward more complex digital analytics.

When we work with nascent retailers, we always conduct a digital strategy assessment to understand where the organization currently stands and where it needs to go. This exercise will help your organization define the purpose of your digital assets. Are you using them to sell products as if they were in a brick-and-mortar store? Are you exclusively an e-commerce business? What other goals do you have for your digital assets in the future, and what strategies are in place to get there?

A digital strategy assessment, looking particularly at the 6 Ps of Digital Transformation, helps nascent retailers begin to understand the areas where they need to improve. They examine their *purpose* for digital measure, the *people* running their marketing and analytics functions, the *processes* driving their decision-making, and the *platforms* they have in place to make it happen.

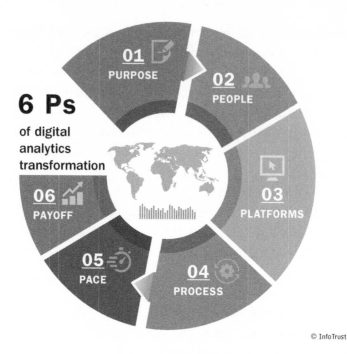

6 Ps
of digital
analytics
transformation

01 PURPOSE
02 PEOPLE
03 PLATFORMS
04 PROCESS
05 PACE
06 PAYOFF

© InfoTrust

Retailers tend to put a lot of emphasis on product placement and understanding consumer engagement on their digital platforms, but there are so many potential products and customer interactions that it can become overwhelming. In terms of purpose, retailers want customers to have a seamless way to find what they need on their websites and complete a purchase. Beyond products and online shopping, they might also have a lot of offers and promotions, possibly seasonal or holiday-related, as they try to stay competitive.

With so many different ways to engage with customers online, where should you focus your efforts to increase engagement? How can you track and manage customer engagement? What process should you use in executing campaigns to make measurement possible? Nascent retails must begin to think through and answer these kinds of questions as they deploy analytics to measure customer activities on their digital assets.

The purpose is not merely to assess where things stand but to determine how they should be set up for optimal success. What is the ideal measurement architecture? Does the current implementation cover all of your reporting needs? What different tools, technologies, and tags are deployed? Is there a platform migration that needs to be deployed to enable people and processes to drive measurement forward?

Some specific tactical deliverables from working with clients in the nascent stage include:

- Deploying a measurement maturity assessment
- Benchmarking against other organizations for where you need to go to grow and migrate to reach the emerging stage
- Building roadmaps and key milestones to enhance digital collection
- Completing a technical audit for what is in place today
- Beginning an implementation and configuration of data collection at the most basic level

To start putting digital analytics in place that will move a retailer from nascent to emerging, there must be a clear purpose for how digital analytics are used. Setting objectives and KPIs, such as *completed purchases* and *products bought*, tied to the specific marketing channels that bring users to the website is a fundamental starting point. With just this data alone, many additional capabilities and insights can be achieved, assuming you're collecting quality data with accuracy (see our customer data governance chapter for more information on accurate data collection).

In later analytics maturity stages, you'll focus on more involved tracking for specific steps in the customer journey, but in the nascent stage, the goal is to start putting tracking elements in place around key conversions and key products being purchased. It's important to deploy platforms and tools that will give your business quick, short-term wins while still developing a long-term roadmap for more robust tracking and more sophisticated analysis down the road.

To progress beyond the nascent stage, the most important milestone you want to reach is the ability to ensure all stakeholders and teams are engaged, able to understand the data, and confident in its accuracy, even if you're only measuring a few KPIs. The team needs to be invested in all of the platforms you've selected for data collection and analysis and comfortable leveraging these tools to optimize marketing against these basic but critical KPIs.

Once your people begin exploring the platforms, processes will develop as curiosity for more data increases. Your goal is to get your whole team seeking more insights from the data, obtaining more knowledge, and identifying more questions. Bear in mind, progressing from nascent to emerging doesn't require full and complete tracking of everything your customers can do online within your digital assets. As long as you are defining and accurately tracking a few key KPIs, you're moving in the right direction.

Just as my son, Charlie, needs to ensure his basic needs are met before he can start learning to crawl, walk, or run, retailers need to start small by getting the fundamentals in place in order to grow and mature. More advanced tracking, along with secondary KPIs, can be captured as your processes develop and you move into higher stages of analytics maturity.

INTEREST AND CURIOSITY: EMERGING RETAILERS

Most parents of young children will tell you that setting a schedule and putting a routine in place helps with a child's stress and health. Charlie has a strict nap schedule, which has helped us get him to sleep through the night, making him a happier baby when he wakes. This, in turn, lets us start thinking through other aspects of his development, such as exercise and spending time on his tummy so he can learn to hold his head up—a key step in eventually learning to walk.

He needs more than just his parents now. In this next stage of development, it's important to have a lot of fun toys to interact with. In a similar way, retailers progressing into the emerging stage already have foundational tracking in place that includes key KPIs and conversion tracking, but now their curiosity begins to mount. People within the organization understand the importance of digital analytics, and they're asking more questions.

A platform upgrade will probably be necessary as the current analytics platform might be too basic. People in the organization are actively engaged with their data, but they still rely heavily on third-party data and outside partners or resources. They're not able to move quickly to the insights they need because external partners and agencies delay action. It takes longer to make data-driven decisions about marketing.

Emerging retailers have initiated analysis and reporting in various departments, but they're largely siloed. Typically, only a few analysts are providing insights for the entire organization, and digital analytics data is not yet a regular part of the marketing or product departments' core decision-making. However, emerging retailers have more engaged team members asking more sophisticated questions that need more sophisticated analytics tracking. This leads to more data collection, more integrated systems, more people involved as stakeholders and end users, and less reliance on outside reporting, vendors, and third-party services. Analytics champions begin to rise in the organization.

To progress further in the emerging stage, it's important to keep building on top of the tracking foundation that was deployed in the nascent stage. Most retailers start out using free technology for digital analytics. This is fine for tracking a few core KPIs, but most emerging organizations outgrow this free tech. They need the service-level agreements and data guarantees that come from advanced tracking.

This is also the stage when retailers begin collecting "in-between" interactions. When someone visits the website, there are the questions that analytics must begin to answer:

- What are the key products that customers are looking at before buying?
- How are they engaging with them?
- Which products are they seeing, which products are they clicking on, and on which product list pages?
- How should the product merchandising and layout appear on category pages or product list pages?
- How should product detail pages be formatted?
- What promotions, offers, and discounts are showing, and how frequently?

Getting all of these measurements in place so you know how customers are interacting on your platforms, engaging with your brands, and which key elements or interactions drive the most conversions is the *most important focus* of the emerging stage.

This is the time to consider upgrading your platform, improving your analytics processes, and training your people more thoroughly. In the emerging stage, you're going to have more measurements, more data processing needs, and you will want to have service-level agreements in place for your digital data collection platforms and vendors. Moving from Google Analytics free edition to Analytics 360 is critical.

Consider engaging with a partner to help you deploy the greater measurement requirements, so your reporting and analysis capabilities are set for the future, tying together your analytics purpose, people, and processes more efficiently.

The extra data collection and deployment provided by an enterprise-level platform also require more customized training support and cross-department business engagement. Using Google Marketing Platform as our example, the enterprise-level software allows deeper integrations with your advertising platforms. For example, Google Analytics integrates directly with Google Ads, Search Ads 360, Campaign Manager, and Display & Video 360, allowing seamless data sharing and advanced audience capabilities (for more information, refer to chapter five).

To get from the emerging stage to the connected stage, measurements will have to become part of your regular decision-making, with more questions focusing on customer engagement and driving business objectives. You'll need to build out your digital analytics deployment and the usage of your enterprise tool, configuring advanced integrations with your other marketing technologies.

A retailer leveraging this integrated data for audience targeting, exploring how to build a more centralized view of customers, and engaging those customers through the data that is being collected, is ready for the next stage of analytics maturity. Just as Charlie has more engagement from his toys and more stimulation from activities now, retailers need to enhance their platforms and process to continue growing as they progress to the connected stage.

KNOWING THE WHOLE STORY: CONNECTED RETAILERS

Every day, my son does something new and amazing, even if it's just a minor improvement like figuring out how to put his hand in his mouth or noticing his own shadow and staring at it. There are so many new interactions in his life, knowing which ones are the most important for his development can be daunting.

It's hard for us to track and understand the importance of all of his new behaviors and activities, but as his parents, we do what we can to help him learn, grow, and develop. To do that, we try to maintain a big-picture view of his behavior in relation to his overall progress, and, of course, we're always trying to learn how to become better parents.

Similarly, retailers in the connected stage are focusing on the overall customer and their interactions, learning how and when to better engage with them. Connected retailers understand the effectiveness of media, and they are able to drive more personalized, engaging campaigns both on-site and off-site through advertising. They're looking for different marketing tests driven by data to test conversion rates, and they've already fully upgraded and implemented a variety of platforms within the Google Marketing Platform.

They have buy-in throughout their organization, with people leveraging data, running analysis, and making decisions about upgrading both systems and approaches. Now, in the connected stage, they're working to get even closer with the customer, exploring more effective ways to drive better customer relationships. They are constantly testing things like product layout, offers and promotions, and navigational pathing for customers. They might be improving checkout flow, using key customer intent data to power experimentation as they test for a lift in conversions.

A key milestone of connected retailers happens when they start to bring in external data, not just the data captured within their digital analytics platform. Now, they've connected to other resources and touchpoints with customers, including integrations with data management platforms, third-party tools, and various channels, which gives them cost and spend data that would otherwise not be available in their analytics platforms.

Retailers selling products with brand partners might not be able to track or capture cost of goods sold, product profits, or other metrics through user interactions on their website. In the connected stage, these organizations will start to automatically integrate this data into their digital analytics platform while continuing to explore ways to optimize their strategies, focusing not just on revenue or products sold, but driving greater product margin and ROI.

Connected retailers explore different advanced attribution models, trying to pinpoint where specific campaigns are most successful. They don't just look at last-click attribution, preferring more sophisticated analysis and insight provided through the integration of their digital analytics tools with external data sources from other channels.

Additional metrics and data points can come from the following, though this is by no means an exhaustive list:

- Email marketing platform
- CRM and customer data platforms
- Product databases and inventories
- Brand partner product pricing and cost of goods sold

A connected retailer begins to organize all of its customer data, both in terms of advertising and on-site engagement, into its measurement platform, so it can power test both on-site and off-site while continuing to drive personalization experiments to its customers.

The final component of a connected retailer is the ability to ensure a consistent, seamless experience for customers as they engage the brand offline (via ads) and online (via on-site configuration). The most powerful way to accomplish this is by integrating and launching a tool like Optimize for A/B testing and personalization connected to your analytics platform. This drives more advanced marketing because, as the name of the stage implies, connected retailers are *connected* with their customers at every stage of the buying journey.

GROWING UP: MULTI-MOMENT RETAILERS

My most special times with Charlie are those moments when his personality shines. These interactions, whether they happen when he first wakes up or in the middle of the night, will live with my wife and me forever. These are the moments when he is most connected with us. After his needs have been met, he is able to experience these beautiful connections with the world around him. It's particularly fun when we test new things, like reading him a new book and letting him try certain foods for the first time.

Of course, as parents, there's a lot of trial and error along the way, but we're learning what resonates the most with Charlie, and we're learning when engagement is most effective. Retailers experience similar moments of genuine connection, turning customers into lifelong advocates when they create these special moments with them. To get there, they have to test different ways of strengthening the relationship to see what works.

Multi-moment retailers have become very good at this. They are the most advanced organizations in terms of digital analytics, and they've become sophisticated marketers and expert analysts. In the multi-moment stage, your organization becomes an analytics machine, optimizing media both automatically and by individual efforts to drive growth for your organization.

A lot of automation is in place for your data flow, and you use predictive modeling effectively. Your organization can start exploring new capabilities and opportunities with your data, launching more comprehensive tests. Since analytics data collection and measurement have been well deployed with clear purpose and the right people, platforms, and processes to activate the data, every decision becomes data-driven. You have confidence exploring new tactics for digital marketing, assured that the data collection is in place to optimize, with support from machine learning algorithms that constantly model the data and provide outputs about what's working or not.

Retailers who reach the multi-moment stage have brought together all of the key developments from earlier stages. They laid down basic foundation tracking in the nascent stage, then they developed enhanced data collection with more prepurchase actions around their product engagement, offers, and on-site behavior in the emerging stage. They connected their marketing and advertising technologies to create a unified, single view of the customer.

They have deployed tests, are running hypothesis and multivariate or personalization experience tests for customers to make sure their on-site experience is connected through their off-site experience, all of it powered by real data. The key difference between a connected and multi-moment retailer, then, is that now there is automation in place with ongoing testing, debugging, and validation of all tracking behind the scenes.

Developers, marketers, or partners don't have to manually check for data quality. Automatic quality checking is firmly in place, with all data being automatically assessed, monitored, and potentially repaired. Retailers can use that data to run predictive models to see which marketing activities yield the most conversions, building lifetime value output. That, in turn, allows them to determine which customers are most valuable to the business so they can drive the right focus in marketing investments.

These data science models predict profitability, reveal where to invest your media, and show you which products are most correlated. For a retail business with many different products, it's important to know which one to bundle, which offers to make at which times, and which promotions or discounts work best during specific seasons.

Multi-moment retailers know all of this. With their predictive analyses, they are able to answer the following questions:

- What are the expected sales—same day or a week from now or even a few months from now—based on the digital analytics and measurement capture that we have?
- How can that influence customer decision-making?
- If I reallocate X investment, what is my expected positive or negative return?

Though machine learning and artificial intelligence are the future of digital analytics, insights, and actionability, retailers still need humans to validate the machine outputs and recommendations, running tests to see what works and what doesn't. However, thanks to automation, multi-moment organizations can stop worrying and spending time on data collection and focus on optimization and engagement instead.

So, how will you know when you've reached multi-moment maturity? What is the ultimate milestone? It's simple. You'll know you're there when your data collection, analyses, and testing processes are fully automated. At that point, you will become more predictive, using data to determine what will happen in the future, and adjusting your activities to drive more growth.

Similarly, there will come a day when Charlie is able to get around on his own. He will gradually become a fully independent human, able to make wise decisions about what is best. As a parent, it's a double-edged sword because kids just grow up too fast! Still, it is the milestone you strive for as a parent, isn't it?

Charles Shawki learning digital analytics.

GOOGLE ANALYTICS 4 FOR RETAILERS

Google Analytics 4 is moving away from the current data collection model and reporting of Universal Analytics. This represents a major shift in analytics, and it will present some significant changes for retailers and e-commerce brands. In the Google Analytics 4 chapter, we looked at the general changes which this new platform is bringing, but now we want to look at what this will mean specifically for retailers.

The biggest change, in terms of product development, is the ability to see all of your data—website, app, and more—in a single, unified, event-based model. Most retailers have a mobile presence, many with specific mobile apps that need to track sales or transactions, as well as a website. In GA4, they will be able to combine the data from these in a much simpler way, creating a clearer and more complete picture of the overall health of the business.

Historically, Google Analytics provided a few ways to merge app and website data, but it required a lot of manual work. Now, however, it is a simple process, thanks to the core event-based model. This should prove especially critical for retailers, as they track their most important metrics: sales and revenue. In turn, this should make analytics far easier.

Previously, in Universal Analytics, it was difficult to answer even some basic questions because data was stored differently depending on the platform. For example, website interactions were tracked as page views, while app interactions were tracked as screen views. Analyzing them together to determine which one was more valuable and efficient was challenging. In GA4, both of these types of interactions are tracked as events, which simplifies tracking from the ground up, *and* simplifies reporting from the top down.

At the same time, GA4 is shifting to a user-centric focus and tracking more e-commerce behaviors. In Universal Analytics, you can track your products down the funnel, but that funnel is very narrow and favors same-session conversion. In GA4, you can track many more e-commerce actions with your products, such as "adding an item to your favorites." A user who "favorites" an item can be tracked across multiple sessions at different times until they convert. The more comprehensive dataset should prove far more valuable for retailers for this and many other reasons because you can now analyze the entire customer journey and aren't limited to a single-session conversion model.

You are able to see all of the little actions a customer makes before they convert—favoriting items, adding them to a wish list, saving an item for later, and so on. You might want to set some of these key e-commerce actions as micro-conversions, so you can drive your marketing efforts toward them. GA4 provides the flexibility to do this, and you can visualize all of that data much easier, which makes it clear how these actions impact conversion over time.

With the changing privacy landscape, it is becoming more difficult for retailers to conduct session-based analyses because it relies on cookies and other identifiers that don't adhere to new privacy regulations. Google Analytics 4 has been built with privacy regulations in mind. Instead of session-based analysis, you can track user identifiers to connect multiple platform interactions together.

With the way the industry is going, the days of anonymous users and tracking cookies are coming to an end anyway, so retailers need to make the mindset shift. They should be focusing on ways to drive interest in their platforms, so customers will create accounts that provide user identifiers that GA4 can use to tie all user activity together across multiple platforms.

The ability to tie user activity together across platforms also enables retailers to provide a more holistic experience for customers. No longer do they have to focus solely on pushing someone down the funnel as fast as possible as soon as they navigate to the website. Now, they can really engage customers in multiple ways, nurturing a relationship that will increase lifetime value and loyalty.

At the same time, Google can run more predictive analytics to find additional insights and serve nuggets of insight automatically. This is called "anomaly detection," and it's a huge value-add for GA4. We're talking about a completely new feature that enables Google to crunch data on a much larger scale than ever before, so they're able to provide more robust capabilities for retailers, marketers, and analysts. Many of these additional machine learning capabilities are available out of the box, which should help retailers move faster from nascent to emerging to connected analytics maturity.

These additional capabilities mean retailers can unlock more sophisticated technology for powering their on-site experiences. For example, the more robust dataset can power your recommendation engines to determine which products are shown in a search grid. Of course, many retailers have already been doing this, but thus far, it has required expensive resources and a lot of development time to make it possible.

WHAT DOES TRANSITION LOOK LIKE?

If you're a retailer, you probably already have an enterprise analytics solution, such as Analytics 360, and you might have already deployed it robustly. Indeed, maybe you're already approaching the connected or multi-moment stage of maturity. If so, the transition to GA4 isn't going to be as simple as flipping a switch and getting the data flowing because you're shifting to an entirely new model, which is event- and user-based rather than session-based.

This gives you the perfect opportunity to refresh your KPIs and processes. As a starting point, we recommend creating a data migration plan where you identify the key KPIs you want to capture. Think carefully about what you want to track for your business, taking into consideration the events, attributes, dimensions, and metrics you're already tracking.

Map all the KPIs you're already tracking, taking your business goals into consideration, and determine what your ideal state would look like. Rather than simply copying everything over from your current platform to GA4, use this transition as a time to assess what you're doing now and what might be missing. This requires having clearly outlined goals, so you might need to spend some time figuring those out.

For example, maybe you set a goal to find little ways to delight customers in order to drive loyalty. With GA4, you will now have a way of tracking all of those little moments. Once you've figured out your goals, create a plan for realizing them. Your tagging might need to change, but this is a chance to start over and create a better implementation to serve your needs. Make the most of it.

At this point, your goals should be clearly identified, you should have decided all of the things you want to capture, and you should have a map of your current setup. As a final step of your transition plan, we recommend implementing a dual-tagging system by deploying GA4 side by side with your existing analytics (e.g., Analytics 360). This will allow you to compare data you're used to seeing against the future of your data and will help you understand the changes taking place in a more tangible way. To do this, you may need to change the current structure of your tag management system.

Depending on your current system, your transition may need to be a multiphase approach that could take up to a year or more, but we recommend getting it done as soon as possible so you can begin collecting year-over-year data. This is going to be a huge shift, and trying to get a handle on everything might seem daunting. The most important aspect of your transition to GA4 is figuring out how to prioritize your e-commerce events so you can get to your bottom line.

• • • •

PART FOUR

MANAGER'S TOOLKIT: WHAT'S NEXT?

CHAPTER ELEVEN

CHASE YOUR VISION

**CHAPTER CONTRIBUTORS: STACEY
SHIRING AND KENT OLDHAM**

 As our Head of Global Client Success, Stacey was invited to coauthor this chapter because of the relationships she builds with the C-suite in helping them to navigate their analytics maturity with our delivery teams. She has experienced firsthand the triumphs and struggles of over a hundred enterprise businesses as they are going through their digital transformations. She works with our team to share what she has learned so we can build improved processes to create seamless transitions in the client journey, creating raving fans.

Stacey spends her time outside of the office working with diverse business owners to help them build stronger businesses by advancing their emotional intelligence and foundations of business. At InfoTrust, she is constantly looking for ways to team-build, from leading our book club to ribbon-dancing for laughs—she has no shortage of ideas.

During a conference in London not long ago, we met with people from a number of organizations, and each of them shared their vastly different experiences with digital transformation, particularly in regard to analytics and innovation.

During one such meeting, an organization showed us a chart of what they were trying to accomplish: their priorities, their overall business capabilities, and how each department specifically contributed to innovation. Everyone in their organization was on the same page, and as a result, there seemed to be a lot of excitement about where they were going. It reminded us of a quote from the movie *The Godfather Part III*: "Our ships must all sail in the same direction."

Sadly, this alignment is rare in most organizations. During that same meeting in London, we asked the people we met with, "What are the priorities of your organization for the next year?" Over and over again, we got blank looks and responses like, "We don't know. That information hasn't been shared with us yet. We're still waiting to hear from the executive team."

It might be tempting to excuse these organizations. Maybe it wasn't the right time of year to set their budgets or determine their priorities for the next year. However, we have heard the exact same responses quarter after quarter from organizations in all sorts of industries. The time of year doesn't seem to matter. Executive teams might have a vision for the future, but people on the frontline don't know it, don't understand it, or can't articulate it clearly. Even if the team has a vague sense of it, they rarely see how it ties into their day-to-day activities.

We can't say this strongly enough: *Alignment of vision at all levels is absolutely essential, especially in a large organization.*

Indeed, without it, you will never reach the multi-moment stage of digital analytics maturity.

Why?

First, the average term of a marketing executive is relatively short, often no more than a couple of years. In many cases, when they leave, their strategy and initiatives get dumped, most of them unfinished. Then a new executive comes in and introduces a whole new set of initiatives and a brand-new strategy. This creates a deadly cycle within the organization where strategy changes every couple of years—nobody knows what the current strategy is, and therefore, no one buys in. Nothing gets fully implemented, and marketing stays in a constant state of half-realized initiatives.

Ideally, when a marketing executive leaves a company, the organization should already have buy-in on an overall marketing strategy, a solid plan in place that is already being implemented, and a commitment to keep it going. The joint effort of the organization should be stronger than any single person.

To align your teams and prioritize your efforts effectively, we recommend a concept called *vivid vision*.

WHAT IS A VIVID VISION?

The concept of *vivid vision* was created by business consultant and bestselling author Cameron Herold.[29] The idea is to create a holistic, big picture of what your company is going to look like in the next three years. You might have some specific goals

---

29   Cameron Herold, *Vivid Vision* (Austin, TX: Lioncrest Publishing, 2018).

that your company is working toward, but what exactly will the organization look like when you get to that point? What will it feel like?

Most company leaders, especially owners, spend their days thinking about the future of the company, but how many team members spend time thinking about where the company will be in three, five, or ten years? If you are like most organizations, probably very few.

A vivid vision brings the entire organization into alignment because every team member knows what they are working toward, and they know that what the company is working toward as a whole fulfills their individual needs. Consequently, team members have the motivation and desire to persist when things get tough (or mundane). They know the bigger picture, and they see the part they play in helping the whole team achieve success.

The vivid vision creates a portal to the future so the team can see and feel how the hard work today will pay off. They see themselves in your innovation lab creating new products every year. Or your digital team works in a cutting-edge building because your growth in innovation has paid off to create a new and exciting environment with supportive leaders. Maybe your future online customer experience is the fastest in the industry and creates raving fan clients that reach out on their own accord to thank you. By doing this, you are visualizing what success will look like and how the day-to-day activities of your various teams will be different, so the team has something to measure against.

Of course, you don't do this one time. We suggest you regularly revisit your vision, tracking your progress in realizing it, so your organization as a whole continues to work together toward a set of common objectives. At InfoTrust, every quarter and every year, leaders realign the organization to the vision to keep everyone moving in the same direction, using vivid vision to define quarterly and annual priorities.

Walk the halls of our company, and you will see our vivid vision framed for all to see. At our quarterly meetings, we print a vivid vision for every member of our team, using one color to highlight the things we've achieved and another color to highlight the things we've not yet achieved. We then talk about what we need to do to stay on track with the next quarter's priorities.

Making the vision present in your day-to-day work, celebrating what has been achieved each quarter, and making a plan for the next quarter will engrain that future vision into the hearts and minds of each person in your organization. Decisions start being influenced by the repetition of common goals that everyone is passionate about achieving. Our 2019 Vivid Vision stated a goal of receiving five cultural awards. You can imagine our excitement as we finished the cycle with four out of five, including *Fortune* magazine's "Best Place to Work."

THIRTY-DAY PLAN

We've covered a lot of information in this book, but digital transformation doesn't happen overnight. You may be wondering where to start, especially if you don't have a specific glaring analytics problem demanding your attention. We encourage you to start with the self-assessment that we shared in chapter two but don't just conduct the self-assessment by yourself. Invite ten to fifteen people in your organization to do it as well so you can compare results. Otherwise, people throughout your organization might have very different ideas about what to prioritize. By comparing results, you can begin to get alignment on one to three things that need to be addressed in the next thirty days. Once you have identified one to three actionable steps, you can begin to clarify and chase a vision.

ALIGNING YOUR ORGANIZATION

How do you get your people to understand and buy in to the vision of the organization? How can you align the efforts of everyone from the frontlines up to the executive suite so that your organization becomes more competent? More specifically, how can this alignment contribute to more effective use of digital analytics that will grow your organization?

The words *digital transformation* are thrown around a lot, and there are endless conversations in marketing about analytics, people, and software, but the core of digital transformation is your leadership and the culture you help create. You can have the latest platforms, amazing dashboards, and clean data, but the companies who excel have strong leadership and a unified culture.

Let's take a look at what a difference two years and a vivid vision can make.

WITHOUT A VISION

A certain partner of ours had a C-suite member with a strong vision that she constantly championed in the organization. By sheer force of will, she pushed through a bunch of changes that needed to happen in order to build an effective analytics department. Then, this C-suite champion left the company, and her initiatives were handed to another C-suite member who lacked the background on these initiatives and time to focus on goals for the coming year, and progress stalled.

Since then, that leadership position has changed several times, and when we last met with the company, they expressed frustration about slow progress and broken promises. The whole team was demoralized, and it showed on their faces.

WITH A VISION

We had another client organization in which the C-suite champion brought her vision to the leadership and got total buy-in from every executive. They built a culture of innovation and experimentation that made room for people to try new things and fail without being embarrassed, and they established transparency around that vision. We cheered them on as their vision came to life and transformed the entire organization.

Google Analytics was given a seat at the table, so they could connect the vision to hard data. The vision was no longer dependent on a single person since each person had ownership and knew how their day-to-day work impacted the future. All ships were sailing in the same direction, and everyone knew where they were going.

Buy-in from a leadership team can make or break digital transformation within an organization. If leaders don't set the right culture, the organization is going to struggle. How do you measure up as a company that embraces innovation, allows experimentation, and allows failure or setbacks? What business practices that your company was founded on need to be tweaked, adjusted, or set aside? There is no room for ambiguity or uncertainty. Leaders must communicate at all levels, and people need to know with 100 percent certainty that their leaders have their backs.

WHAT IS YOUR WHY?

Simon Sinek is famous for saying, "People don't buy what you do; they buy why you do it." If you want buy-in across your organization, you have to communicate your why clearly.

"We're doing this to get cheaper clicks on our website." That's not really a why, and it certainly doesn't inspire an audience. To define your why, you have to connect the dots between your digital analytics and how they make your business better.

Yes, you're trying to solve problems with website performance, reduce your cost of acquisition, and all sorts of things, but your why isn't really about any of those. It's about the reason your business wants to exist. How are you making the lives of customers better? How are you making things easier for them?

If your organization can't answer these kinds of questions at a senior level, you're going to have a hard time communicating a vivid vision to people in the organization who are responsible for doing the actual work of making it happen.

In too many organizations, there is a sense of competing priorities. On an individual level, people are competing for promotions. Teams are working in their own little silos. Nobody is really clear on how teams are supposed to interact or who is in charge. We hear confusion coming out of many organizations:

"I had no idea the other team was responsible for this."

"Are we supposed to be using a different platform? I didn't know we had the license for it."

"Which team are we supposed to be working with on this initiative?"

All of this confusion and all of the competing priorities create inefficiencies. The lack of clarity becomes a challenge in anything the organization wants to accomplish. Different teams are trying to solve the same problems independently of one another. When a team accomplishes something, starts some new initiative, or selects a new product, they fail to communicate it to the broad organization. Consequently, other teams are slow to learn about the change—if they ever learn at all.

Digital transformation is simply not going to succeed in this kind of environment. The what and the why of any decision needs to be communicated throughout the entire organization.

COMMUNICATING YOUR VISION

A unified vision contributes to change management. Let's suppose you decide to switch from one marketing platform to another. You need to communicate to your organization why this change is happening, what improvements it will make, why it matters, and address their fears. You also need to clearly communicate your expectations of team members regarding the new platform.

How soon do you expect them to be able to use the new platform? Are you going to upskill them? What's the time frame in which they will be expected to become proficient at it? If they fail to meet that timeline, what will the consequences be?

It's part of your broader effort of communicating your vivid vision for the organization. When you can tell people plainly what the company wants to achieve in upcoming years and why, creating a vivid vision of what it will look like, you set your teams up for success. They know what they are aiming for. They understand what is expected of them. They know why they're doing it, even if they don't yet know the exact steps they're going to take to get there.

Leadership must provide the necessary training for any upscaling. Who are the mentors your team members can turn to? What benchmarks and milestones will they need to meet?

When you implement change without vision, particularly some big innovation that is meant to drive your business forward, people are going to be afraid. If you bring in a new platform, for example, some are going to wonder, "Will I be let go because of this product?"

We've seen situations where a company introduced a new product, and people said, "I'll hold out on learning this new platform because it'll probably go away or get replaced in a few months." That leads to the product being underutilized, so then, in a self-fulfilling prophecy, company leaders say, "No one's using this product, so clearly it's not going to accomplish what we wanted it to. Let's go find a new product to replace it." It's a vicious cycle.

IT'S WORTH THE TIME

Maybe you're reading this and thinking, "On top of everything else we're doing at our company, we just don't have the time to create and promote a vivid vision." The truth is, not only do you have the time, but you can't afford *not* to create a vision for the future. It's an extremely competitive landscape out there, and companies are going out of business every year. Digital transformation can be the end of your business if you don't get it right.

The technology by itself isn't going to save you. Adding another dashboard won't align your teams and get you moving in the right direction. If you can't get team buy-in, if you can't get them to support your transformation, it's not going to succeed. Even in a good economy, without a vivid vision, your people won't stick around long enough to see it come together. When there's competition for talent, people will look for a company that is exciting to work for.

When we talk to partners about why they like to go to work, they rarely mention a perk. "Oh, I love the catered lunches they provide." Everyone enjoys perks and benefits, but what really makes people want to come to work is feeling like they are truly part of a team and working together toward a common goal. An aligned team is an excited team, and that is where innovation, collaboration, and growth flourish.

When you have a vivid vision, it also helps create the right culture to truly implement organization-wide transformation. People rarely like change when it feels haphazard or when it is implemented without a clear purpose. However, if they understand the vision behind the change, if they can see and feel the road ahead, and if they're working in an environment with a healthy culture, they are more likely to embrace it.

CHAPTER TWELVE

MANAGING UNCERTAINTY

Almost every time we start working with a large organization, at least one member of their team will say, "We're notorious for making decisions slowly." Large organizations generally have a reputation for not being fast or agile. Whether or not the stereotype is true, decision-making in a large organization certainly involves a lot of complex considerations since every decision has the potential to impact numerous teams and individuals. To avoid unintended consequences, you need a good process in place to make decisions wisely.

When you have a lot of moving pieces in your organization, you also have many priorities. Even if you're a small organization, there are about a hundred different ways you can try to improve. It's very easy to simply pick one of those ways, almost at random, and say, "Yes, let's do that."

What differentiates successful companies from struggling companies is the ability to determine what to focus on and what to set aside. A few years ago, when Yahoo! was run by ex-Google exec Marissa Mayer, the company went through a significant redesign, created a new logo, acquired Tumblr, and pursued many other interesting initiatives. Despite this, it's hard to think of one single thing that they did exceptionally well. It might be fair to conclude that they made too many decisions and pursued too many things.

On the other hand, look at what Facebook did during the same period of time. They realized users were moving from desktop to mobile, so they decided to focus on creating a mobile experience. Mark Zuckerberg held regular meetings to champion the cause. He knew that if they didn't get this one thing right, everything else might fail. While there are plenty of ways you can criticize Facebook's decisions, their focus on moving to mobile worked.

Instead of trying to pursue every initiative or select one at random, figure out what the key decisions are that will either make or break the company. Be willing to pass on decisions that aren't likely to matter in the long run. Those are traits of great leadership and a great organization.

ERRATIC CUSTOMER BEHAVIOR

Leaders often struggle to make decisions because of imperfect customer data, but customer behavior will always be hectic. Therefore, customer data will always be imperfect. Think about the average journey of a customer deciding to buy a mattress online. They visit a website and look at the prices. Then they visit another website, check those prices, and maybe read some product descriptions. Later, they might visit an actual brick-and-mortar store and test a product in person. Then they come home, read a few mattress reviews, watch some YouTube videos, and finally decide to go on Amazon and buy the mattress they tested in-store.

Connecting the dots on such erratic behavior is nearly impossible. The customer experience will never be perfect or entirely predictable, no matter how much you improve your online customer experience. If anything, it will only get worse as privacy regulations make customer behavior harder to track.

In this environment, we see a rising number of company leaders suffering from *analysis paralysis*. The simple fact is this: you have to be willing to make decisions without perfect data.

PLACING SMALL BETS

Instead of seeking perfect data before making a decision, determine the *minimum threshold* of data you need to make smart decisions. Maybe you've experienced that all-too-common nightmare scenario of spending a few million dollars to run a big data integration project only to learn a few years down the road that the project doesn't meet the initial requirements. Maybe it's such a long-term project that no one even remembers the full list of requirements by the end.

This kind of experience can be profoundly disheartening and contribute to analysis paralysis for future decisions. In order to make big, long-term decisions with confidence, we recommend placing numerous small bets and seeing how they pay off. In turn, those will help you make better "big bet" decisions. After all, you only know a decision was right once you see the metrics or outcomes, and making small bets provides that vital feedback.

This is why large corporations developed the concept of the

minimum viable product. Rather than putting time and money into a finished product that may or may not sell, they test the first iteration of the product for feedback.

Instead of waiting a couple of years for feedback about a big integration project, which might outlast the tenure of your CMO, test the quality of that decision along the way. Receive small amounts of continual feedback and apply it to your big decision.

Ideally, you want good decision-making to become a habit. When you are regularly analyzing data and applying it to your decisions, you are developing that habit. Look at the available data, make a decision, learn from that decision, and make a better decision—do this over and over, and you won't have to rely on gut feelings or guesswork. The feedback loop of *test*, *analyze data*, *apply* needs to become ingrained in the company culture from the top all the way down.

The Digital Analytics Feedback Loop

THE IMPORTANCE OF NEW VOICES

At InfoTrust, we're big proponents of introducing new voices. So many organizations we work with in the digital space make decisions based entirely on their own experiences. They don't like outside voices and prefer to do everything by themselves. Of course, having confidence that your organization can accomplish great things is fine, but if you never listen to voices outside of your organization, industry, or environment, you can develop an insular view.

Learning about the perspectives and experiences of others provides further feedback that can give you a broader and more accurate picture of what is going on. Even the experiences of people in different industries can provide useful information for your decision-making process.

Procter & Gamble made news in 2016 when they started proactively hiring people from outside rather than promoting from within for senior positions.[30] They realized the value of different worldviews, and they wanted to bring those broader experiences into the company. Of course, they were careful with hiring executives from outside on the digital side, but, nevertheless, they wanted to hear from new people.

In particular, they wanted to bring in people with viewpoints or expertise that weren't developed within a large enterprise, people who could provide a powerful comparison contrast for decision-making.

New voices don't necessarily have to be *hired*. You can also

---

30 Jack Neff, "P&G Will Hire More from Outside, Including Marketers, New CEO Says," *AdAge*, February 18, 2016, https://adage.com/article/cmo-strategy/p-g-hire-including-marketers/302739.

leverage your network of peers or third-party organizations to get external viewpoints.

MITIGATION PLAN

Any time you make a decision, we strongly recommend creating a mitigation plan. Too often, organizations make a decision, hoping and planning for success, without a solid plan in place in case it fails. If your decision doesn't go according to plan, you need a good methodology for dealing with possible side effects and consequences. This should always be part of the discussion. Predict the downside and have next steps in place in case it happens.

A mitigation plan should clearly identify risks the business will encounter, particularly in response to strategic decisions, and outline the processes that will be implemented to reduce or eliminate the damage. This might include data governance mistakes, a poor response to a marketing campaign, a bad hire, computer security problems, even transition and succession risks.

If you don't plan for your response, your team might become paralyzed when things go badly. However, if you've outlined clear processes for mitigating the damage, then every member of your team will know how to respond, and they will feel more confident making bold decisions.

FRAMEWORKS FOR DECISION-MAKING

There's no way to make good decisions consistently unless you have an effective decision-making process in place. At Info-Trust, we like the PACE framework, in which you identify the *process owner*, the *approver*, the *contributors*, and the *executors* of a decision.

When a major decision needs to be made, your process owner determines who the contributors will be and who will take ultimate responsibility for making the decision (the approver). Selecting the right approver is always the hardest part in a large enterprise because, typically, you will have many contributors who *believe* they are approvers. However, there should only ever be one approver for any particular decision.

Contributors need to understand that they are providing input to the decision-maker, but they don't get to make the decision themselves. Once the approver makes the decision, the executors are responsible for implementing it.

The Eisenhower Matrix is a popular model for determining *which* decisions to make and is the one Kent uses with his three sons—two college students and one high schooler—to help them get the most out of their time at school. Kent makes sure that Zach, Max, and Clayton fully understand that the bottom right is the enemy of good grades. Every potential decision is placed in one of four quadrants:

- Top Left: for immediate and urgent deadlines.
- Top Right: for long-term strategy and development.
- Bottom Left: for distractions that aren't really important, even though someone wants it now. You can delegate these tasks to someone else.
- Bottom Right: for activities that yield little value and potentially take time away from important activities—the ones Kent works with his sons to stay away from.

Kent Oldham and his three sons Clayton, Max, and Zach.

These two frameworks will help you develop a culture of decision-making within your organization. You will be able to make important decisions faster because you give them more attention, listen to new voices, have a mitigation plan in place, and have frameworks for the decision-making process that eliminate wasted time.

The Eisenhower Matrix

	URGENT	NOT URGENT
IMPORTANT	**DO** it today	**SCHEDULE** a time for it
NOT IMPORTANT	**DELEGATE** it to someone else	**ELIMINATE** stop doing this

© InfoTrust

THEORY OF CONSTRAINTS

The theory of constraints (TOC) is a management philosophy developed by management guru Eliyahu Goldratt and first presented in his book *The Goal*. Anytime you're faced with a decision, you will have at least one *constraint* which prevents you from achieving your goal. A constraint is a weak link in the chain, and it could be a person, a process, a platform, a policy, equipment, or many other things.

TOC provides a way to focus on and deal with these constraints in order to keep everyone moving toward a common goal using a five-step framework (the Five Focusing Steps):

- Focusing Step 1: Identify the system's constraint. It's impossible to manage a constraint unless you know what it is.
- Focusing Step 2: Decide how you're going to exploit the system's constraint to squeeze as much as possible out of

it, maximizing its productivity. After all, a chain is only as strong as its weakest link, so make the weak link as strong as possible.

- Focusing Step 3: Subordinate everything else to the above decision. Avoid producing more than your constraint can handle. Since it is the most limiting aspect of your system, provide it with enough resources to fully utilize it.
- Focusing Step 4: Elevate the constraint. Once the productivity of the constraint has been exhausted, invest in additional resources to increase throughput, but don't gloss over step 3. Some companies jump from step 2 to step 4.
- Focusing Step 5: Prevent inertia from becoming the constraint! Once elevated, your constraint may become stronger and cease being the weakest link. At that point, a new constraint may emerge, so return to step 1 and deal with the new constraint.[31]

In some of the more effective organizations we've worked with, leaders won't make a decision until they have a diagram of constraints. Creating that diagram forces the team to think through their objective and the challenges in realizing it. With the weakest link or links identified, the leader feels more confident about making a decision.

The Theory of Constraints is a tool we've found useful in our organization, as well as part of creating a culture of decision-making. Being able to identify and deal with weak links in the chain of people, processes, and platforms enable leaders to make good decisions faster. More than that, it allows organizations to keep moving toward their objective even in the face of severe challenges.

---

31   Dr. Eliyahu Goldratt, "The Five Focusing Steps (POOGI)," *Theory of Constraints Institute*, accessed January 4, 2020, https://www.tocinstitute.org/five-focusing-steps.html.

WHEN IS A BAD DECISION BAD?

A decision that doesn't lead to the outcome you wanted isn't necessarily a bad decision. Maybe you implement a new type of personalization on your platform, but customers don't respond to it. Does that mean it was a bad decision to implement it? No, not if it provides feedback that improves future decisions and implementations.

What makes something a bad decision is not knowing what to learn from it. Even accomplishing your objective can be a mistake if you don't learn anything. In the end, great decision-making moves your organization in the right direction not only by achieving your goals but also by improving your future efforts.

Sometimes, leaders avoid making a decision one way or the other about something because they don't want to upset people. They don't want to rock the boat, but strong leaders *have* to rock the boat. You can't please everyone, so you just have to operate with the right intentions and the best available data, even if some strongly disagree. If you're creating a culture of decision-making and putting in place an analytics feedback loop of continual improvement, you can rest assured that you will get better at making even the toughest decisions.

CHAPTER THIRTEEN

WHERE ARE WE GOING?

CHAPTER CONTRIBUTORS:
KENT OLDHAM AND AMIN SHAWKI

What do the next few years hold for the world of digital analytics? Data privacy and tag governance are already changing with the rise of restrictive regulations, as we've discussed. The rules of the game continue to evolve in regard to data collection and the use of cookies. What are the other trends that will change the game for digital analytics?

As we put this book together, I sat down with Kent Oldham, our Head of Customer Data Governance, and Amin Shawki, our Head of Growth, to discover what the next few years might have in store for the world of digital analytics. This chapter represents both a summation and exploration of what we see on the near horizon.

However, we won't be focusing on new platforms. Too often,

a discussion of the future boils down to, "Which new tech products should we buy in the coming year?" Instead, we want to look at how digital analytics is changing the way we all do business.

New tools come along every year. If you only think about what new technology you should invest in, you will miss out on some of the more significant trends that are transforming even the fundamentals. Therefore, as we explore some of the areas of change, we want to concentrate chiefly on your people and processes. This is where you're going to see some of the most significant transformations to the digital analytics landscape, and you'd better be ready to embrace the changes if you want to thrive.

EMBRACING THE ANALYTICS AGE

In the end, what is the purpose of digital analytics? We believe its primary purpose is to give companies confidence in decision-making. When you get digital analytics to work for you, you can make informed decisions, building better connections with your customers, and improving your business overall.

Before the digital age, it was very hard to get a picture of the customer journey, to determine what influenced engagement and purchasing decisions, without rounding up a bunch of customers and asking them directly. Digital analytics changed the game, and our happiest clients are those who have figured out how to make it work for them.

The research company Gartner[32] conducted a study recently on

---

32   Rob van der Meulen, "Gartner Analysis of 1H18 U.S. Earnings Calls Reveals Cross-Industry Trends," November 12, 2018, https://www.gartner.com/en/newsroom/press-releases/2018-11-12-gartner-analysis-of-1h18-us-earnings-calls-reveals-cross-industry-trends.

how often executives talk about digital analytics during earnings calls. Notably, those companies that mention it more often tend to outperform those that mention it less. There seems to be a direct, demonstrable connection between good business decision-making and digital analytics.[33]

Indeed, we're starting to see business models transformed by digital analytics, particularly in the US. Media outlets are adjusting their reporting based on real-time analytics feedback, as they are able to see what's working and what isn't working. This is changing the entire media landscape.

"Where attention goes, the energy flows," as the expression says. More organizations are focusing on analytics, and there's a marked increase in data-driven decision-making. However, another relevant expression is, "Garbage in, garbage out." The quality of the data matters, so we believe there will be an increasing focus on *data quality management* in the coming years. Organizations will strive to understand the attributes of good data as they attempt to implement better data quality control.

Of course, there's no such thing as a perfect dataset, and this pursuit of better data can slow companies down. They're striving for a perfection that doesn't exist rather than working on what's already available to them. We see more companies trying to use machine learning and automation to eliminate human errors completely, but in the process, they are causing delays in their decision process. In this environment, human analysts will need to focus more on data quality.

---

33   Samantha Ann Schwartz, "Kraft Heinz's Place in the Market Dropped. Its CIO Is Using Data to Lift It," January 23, 2020, https://www.ciodive.com/news/kraft-heinz-cio-data-analytics/570165/.

With limits being placed on third-party data, due in large part to the rise of privacy regulations, we're going to see a shift back to first-party data, but that could also mean a shift to *higher quality* data. Privacy regulations aren't going away. This is the world we have to operate in now, and the sooner we embrace the change, the better our companies will thrive.

Instead of complaining that the attribution model is dying or pining for the earlier days of lawless data collection, we must move boldly into this *new norm*. Using first-party data and getting customers to self-identify by providing value, such as reward and loyalty programs, will be more important than ever.

UPSKILLING YOUR PEOPLE

There's a rise in machine learning and automation as organizations try to figure out what data is available to them. Indeed, the real power of machine learning comes from its ability to help us make predictions about future customer engagement, so we know what to expect, how customers will behave, which campaigns are most likely to work, and how to grow first-party data.

With more and more automation, the role of data analysts and data scientists is likely to change. Much of what they currently do—identifying missing data, forecasting, data crunching—is being taken over by machine learning algorithms. As a result, we may see a future where they shift from *predictive* analytics to *prescriptive* analytics, as they play a more significant role in making recommendations about what to do with the data.

In a sense, they may become like doctors. Why do you go to a doctor, after all? You don't go there simply to learn what medical conditions you have.

"Well, you have hypertension, and your cholesterol is 240. Now you know. Make of that what you will. Have a nice day!"

No, you go to the doctor because you want a medical expert to look at your health dataset and make recommendations for the best course of action: maybe diet and exercise, medication, possibly surgery.

In the near future, we believe this will be the role of data analysts. They will look at the information and offer possible course corrections: "Here is what we should be doing on Instagram. Here is what we should be doing on Facebook. Here is what needs to change about our mobile analytics."

Once organizations have access to the dataset, prescriptive analytics helps them make the best decisions based on that data. Indeed, as our Head of Customer Data Governance, Kent Oldham suggests, we may find data analysts operating across a spectrum. Some will be training the machine algorithms to make predictions. Others will be taking the AI output and helping companies make decisions.

This is going to demand new skillsets, so it will be important for organizations to offer boot camps for digital analytics training. Some of our partner organizations put their data analysts through classes with exams to make sure they have the right knowledge before they can access the data. However you decide to do it, you need to find ways to empower your analysts to go beyond crunching numbers, so they can interpret the data and impact the decisions of various marketing syndicates in your company.

If you want to be successful at training your analysts to interpret the data, your training will have to focus on improving their critical thinking. How they interpret reports and dashboards will become more important than simply tracking conversion rate or bounce rate. In a sense, they will become both marketers *and* analysts, providing focus for individual teams and departments.

Already, we're seeing departments, roles, and responsibilities blending together as analysts are empowered to contribute more to marketing meetings. The creation of hybrid analyst roles will only become more common—and more valuable— over the next few years. Existing analysts will have to adapt quickly, learning additional skillsets to work effectively in this new blended environment. The word we're hearing more often is *upskilling*, as new skills are tied to old skills to help companies make better decisions with data.

TRANSPARENT PROCESSES

As customer data governance regulations and browser changes bring restrictions to tracking, we're also seeing a change in the nature of the business/customer relationship. First, rather than simply fulfilling direct needs, consumers these days like to buy from companies that they feel personally connected to.

One way companies are doing this in the changing analytics environment is by empowering consumers with their data. Through open-book reporting, smart companies gain a competitive edge by going beyond regulatory minimums to reveal the full extent of their data collection. Just as publicly traded companies post their financial data, more companies will begin to post their analytics data in order to gain consumer trust.

It might sound crazy. After all, you don't want your competitors to know your number of site visitors, conversions, or engagement. Nevertheless, customers expect transparency, so companies that move to open-book reporting on digital metrics will be at an advantage.

Beyond transparency, sharing your digital metrics can also help refocus your organization on the things that matter most. We find that many companies still focus largely on transactions when it comes to their customer relationships. They think primarily about metrics like revenue month-over-month or conversions.

Those metrics matter. However, it has become far more important to make sure you are attracting the *right kind of customers*. You can run a massive sale and accrue plenty of transactions, but that doesn't mean you are attracting the customers you need for long-term growth and success. Over the next few years, we hope to see companies getting more granular about their customer metrics, even as they become more transparent about that information.

Transparency is only going to become more important, and it's going to hit organizations on at least two fronts. Consumers expect transparency of your intents. "What data are you collecting about me, why are you collecting it, and what are you going to do with it? What value exchange can you offer me for my data?" At the same time, consumers want transparency about the products they buy: the supply chain, ingredients, working conditions, and so on.

Companies that embrace both fronts will have an edge in the next few years. We recommend becoming proactive in your digital analytics. Understand where the transparency conversation is going and make the move.

Almost any restaurant you walk into these days provides nutritional information about all of their food. Sometimes, it's prominently posted on the wall. Other times, it's contained in the menu. At one time, this would have been unthinkable, but customers demanded it, and smart companies embraced it.

Transparency also inspired other changes. For example, along with providing nutritional information, McDonald's began to introduce healthy menu options. They saw a shift in customer behavior and met a changing demand. That is the heart of proactive analytics.

HUMANIZING THE DATA

Of course, transparency is not just about posting numbers. You have to humanize them. Look at these two analytics reports:

Our conversion rate has dropped 30 percent, and as a result, we lost $1 million in sales.

Those numbers represent the cold hard facts, but they don't create a human scenario that can be visualized. What if we told a story instead?

Mary saw our advertisement on social media and liked the product features. She followed the link to our website, but when she got to the product page, she realized that some of the promised features in the ad were not actually available on the webpage. To make matters worse, she accessed our website from her mobile device, and it took three seconds to scroll all the way to the bottom of the page to find the advertised product. What can we do to make Mary's life easier?

Which of these reports is more impactful? More importantly, which of them makes it easier to solve an actual customer problem? It is simple to share the numbers, but humanizing the data connects it to real people. Companies are beginning to realize this, and we see more and more of them striving to humanize their data.

Of course, Mary's experience can't reflect the experiences of all of your customers, so you need to combine both the numbers and the stories. Here's an example of how that might look:

> Our mobile conversion rate dropped 5 percent this year. Why are we losing this segment of our customer base? What sort of experiences, or lack of experiences, are driving them away? Let's consider Mary's story, which provides an example of a common problem customers are experiencing on our website.

You don't have to present every single possible customer problem as an individual story. You're just using storytelling to humanize the numbers in a way that makes problem-solving easier. Share the impact of the numbers on real people, and you clarify the pain points.

At the beginning of this chapter, we said the job of analytics is to give organizations confidence about their decision-making. However, as a direct outflow of that purpose, it is also the job of analytics to improve the customer relationship. Machine learning can give you plenty of reports and dashboards, but it can't tell stories about the people behind those numbers. That's your job!

CRAWLING, WALKING, AND RUNNING INTO THE FUTURE

These are just a few of the trends that we see transforming the landscape of digital analytics over the next few years. The challenge for any company is to develop a concrete plan for analytics growth and maturity. Fortunately, you don't have to reinvent the wheel to become effective at analytics. You also don't have to cobble together some half-realized analytics processes.

We've provided you with two frameworks that work well together to help you move in the right direction. By leveraging the 6 Ps of Digital Analytics Transformation, you can begin to move along the Boston Consulting Group's Four Stages of Digital Analytics Maturity. In doing so, you will be well-poised to navigate the massive changes that are, even now, altering the way we all do business.

If you're new at this, don't try to run right out of the gate. Remember, you have to learn to crawl before you can learn to walk. Define your purpose, bring together the right people, platforms, and processes, and be mindful of the pace and payoff. Begin consistently implementing changes and leveraging the tools we've discussed in this book, and you will be well on your way toward digital analytics maturity.

CONCLUSION

When a company that was once on the Fortune 500 list goes bankrupt, nobody says, "They failed because their analytics were bad." Instead, they say, "Somewhere along the way, the company failed to meet the needs of their ideal customer." However, in a very real sense, that *is* analytics.

We've looked at the restrictions, hindrances, and complexities that make analytics more challenging than ever. We've explored the ways you can leverage the 6 Ps in order to grow through the stages of digital analytics maturity.

As we put this book together, a few people asked us, "Why would you write a book on digital analytics that is likely to be inaccurate in six months?" Yes, the industry is changing rapidly, and digital analytics will continue to evolve. Nevertheless, as the tools evolve, the problems that analytics intends to solve remain the same. No matter what happens, you will still need to bring together the right people, processes, and platforms in order to collect, analyze, and use customer data to make the biggest impact on your customer experience.

Even as you spend less time configuring dashboards, you still need to spend time analyzing the information, interpreting it, and applying it correctly to your organization. For analytics teams, the real challenge is presenting the data to the rest of the organization, particularly leaders, in a way they can understand. Data is power, but if you can't communicate it effectively, you won't be able to influence decision-making.

In far too many organizations, executives don't even look at the analytics charts. They rely on their team, and the team doesn't do a good job of interpreting analytics data in a way that is compelling. Mountains of data are useless if you don't know how to interpret them. The data alone won't tell you what to do. To derive meaning from the data, you have to ask better questions.

Don't be afraid to ask questions, explore, try new things, and turn the data inside out. This is the job of a true data analyst. The future belongs to the curious.

By now, you might be a little stressed out about all of the work you have to do to get your analytics architecture in order. If you're in the nascent stage, the necessary steps to get to emerging, connected, and multi-moment might seem overwhelming. Don't get too caught up in the low-level technical details. Leave that to your technical team, whether they are in-house or a third-party partner. Your primary focus should be on the actual business outcomes you're going after.

Technical capabilities aren't a strategy. Remember your vivid vision! What are you building for your customers? That's your true north. Get your team on the same page, moving in the right direction, and start making progress in your digital transformation.

APPENDIX

INFOTRUST

InfoTrust is a global end-to-end digital analytics consulting, data governance, and technology company. A certified Google Marketing Platform Sales Partner and Google Cloud Partner, InfoTrust works with many of the world's most recognizable brands. From Los Angeles to Dubai, they specialize in online measurement architecture for multi-brand companies, breaking down silos and validating data to ensure teams have the confidence to make data-backed decisions for their businesses. Their team specializes in serving three primary industries: consumer packaged goods (CPG), retail, and news and media. InfoTrust does not sell media or execute advertising campaigns and can, therefore, serve as an unbiased analytics partner. Above all, they give brands the confidence they need to make data-backed decisions.

ABOUT TAG INSPECTOR

Tag Inspector is a tag auditing and monitoring platform which drives the tag governance program of hundreds of enterprises globally. With an industry-leading library of classified tags, it gives organizations visibility into what tags are loading, how each tag loads, and the data collected by each on every page across all digital properties. Leveraging the insights gained from Tag Inspector, enterprises can evaluate data collection practices in light of privacy regulations, define their tag governance policy, and monitor adherence to their policies in real time. Tag Inspector was created by the product engineering team at InfoTrust to meet the needs of their multi-brand enterprise clients who were struggling to monitor the accuracy of their data collection across hundreds of websites. Today, Tag Inspector is used across thousands of websites around the world.

INFOTRUST FOUNDATION

Giving back to the community is more than just something InfoTrust does, it's a core part of their culture. Businesses hold a unique opportunity to leverage growth as a way to give back to local and global communities. At InfoTrust, growth not only benefits the company but allows them to give back on an increasingly wider scale. Each employee takes part in the InfoTrust Foundation's mission by dedicating time quarterly and on an as-needed basis to charity events and drives. The InfoTrust Foundation is committed to serving a variety of local and global causes via external nonprofits and establishing their own programs, such as Basket Brigade. "Our success is someone else's miracle."

How can they build an organization where success becomes someone else's miracle? They are proud to say that their 2025 BHAG (Big Hairy Audacious Goal) is to grow InfoTrust into an organization that can donate $1,000,000 per year to InfoTrust Foundation. All proceeds from this book will be part of that donation.

ACKNOWLEDGMENTS

ALEX YASTREBENETSKY

I would like to thank all of our contributors. One day we will figure out how to include thirteen authors in one book! Thank you for the opportunity to learn from all of you. You are true professionals in all you do and amazing human beings and leaders. Thank you:

Amin Shawki
Andy Gibson
Ariel Opelt
Brad Prenger
Bryan Lamb
Chris Vaughan
Kent Oldham
Lucas Long
Melanie Bowles
Michelle Pliskin
Pam Castricone
Stacey Shiring
Tyler Blatt

Nothing has changed or influenced my life more than the birth of my three children, and I want to thank them not just for being amazing gifts but for opening my eyes to so many things I did not know or realize, and turning me into a lifelong advocate for things I am now so passionate to support and influence.

To my wife, Karina. I love you, I worship you, I will take care of you forever.

To my parents and my aunt and uncle for instilling in me an insatiable hunger for learning, as well as an unshakeable faith and confidence that any difficulties can be overcome.

To Michael, my coauthor, for constantly pushing me to be a better version of myself.

To Libora and Sandy, who taught me that nothing is impossible when you have love, faith, and mission.

To Art, who was the first to introduce me to the principles and the importance of diversity, inclusion, and equality.

To Abie, for teaching me about service to others and interreligious dialog.

To Brent and David, who helped lay the foundation of learning what it means to really care for the people I work with.

I want to thank our entire InfoTrust team for choosing to spend what I hope are some of the best years of your career working together. With all of your amazing talent and expertise, you all have countless opportunities, and I never take any of you for granted.

My acknowledgments would not be complete if I did not share the role the Entrepreneurs' Organization has played in my life. I never set out to be an entrepreneur. For over three generations, my family only produced doctors and scientists. I had no education or training in entrepreneurship, only a burning desire to make a mark on this world and build the best place to work. To say that almost everything I know about being a business owner I learned as a result of being a member of the Entrepreneurs' Organization is an understatement. I am so grateful to Verne Harnish for starting this crazy tribe over thirty years ago and launching the Entrepreneurs' Master's Program/Birthing of Giants at MIT.

I would like to thank my EMP class of 2018/ROM 2019 and Brian, our fearless organizer. You are all incredible entrepreneurs and leaders, and I am so grateful for the opportunity to continue learning from all of you.

Thank you, Cameron, for helping me understand the art and science of building a culture.

Jeff, you taught me the most important lesson as an entrepreneur: our success must become someone else's miracle.

To my two forums: thank you for keeping me honest, for challenging me, and for helping me grow.

Last but so not least, I would like to thank the Scribe Media team and JT, in particular. I very much appreciate your commitment, amazing professionalism, and attention to detail. JT, you set the standard for how to be a leader, and I am honored to call you my friend.

MICHAEL LOBAN

I would like to acknowledge the following people:

My parents, who made the decision to immigrate to the United States and give me the opportunity for a better future.

Alex and all of our coauthors, who not only brought their wisdom and ideas to this book but worked relentlessly to put it all together.

The entire InfoTrust team, who inspire me to grow and be more impactful in my decisions and actions.

Laurie Kyser, Sharen Phillips, Jeremy Woodlee, Paul Limbrey, and the entire Google Marketing Platform Partner Team for supporting and growing our partnership.

Neil Hoyne, for always sharing his knowledge and ideas, helping me expand my own thinking.

The InfoTrust advisory board—Jeff Lloyd, Tarek Kamil, Tarita Preston, Tim Butler, and Stacey Browning for ongoing guidance and sharing their business acumen to help us grow and recognize possible challenges before they even arise.

Dr. Art Shriberg, for mentoring me through the years and inviting me to contribute to his book, *Practicing Leadership*.

Abie Ingber, for friendship, mentorship, and living a life of service. Your stories always leave me in awe.

Dr. James Buchanan, for being a true Renaissance man of our

generation. Your Brueggeman Fellowship has been the most profound university experience.

Michael Bernoff, for teaching me how to be a better communicator.

ABOUT THE AUTHORS

ALEX YASTREBENETSKY is CEO and Co-Founder of InfoTrust, a global analytics consulting and data governance company. Under his leadership, InfoTrust has received numerous honors and awards, with inclusions on *Fortune's* Best Small Workplaces, *Ad Age's* Best Places to Work, *The Inc.'s* 5000, and *Inc.'s* Best Workplaces.

MICHAEL LOBAN is Chief Growth Officer at InfoTrust. He's an adjunct instructor at the University of Cincinnati and Xavier University, and is also a presenter and author, with work published in *Forbes*, *AdWeek*, and *CIO* magazine.